Acknowledgements

American Ballet Theatre graciously acknowledges the generous support of Lewis S. Ranieri, Rod Brayman, Brian J. Heidtke and Gage Bush Englund for their leadership of this national initiative.

Our deepest gratitude to Dr. Gary I. Wadler for his outstanding leadership as the Chair of the Medical Advisory Board, along with Julie Daugherty, Peter Marshall, Dr. William G. Hamilton, Dr. Phillip A. Bauman and the Medical Advisory Board.

This project would not have been possible without the commitment and patience of Kate Lydon and Salvatore Garguilo. Thank you for your perseverance.

Special thanks to the following members of ABT's Department of Education & Training for their dedication to bringing this project to fruition: Molly Schnyder, Rebecca Schwartz and Dana Boll.

ABT would also like to acknowledge Audrey Rohan, Esq. and Marya Lenn Yee, Esq. for their invaluable legal expertise.

Finally, ABT is grateful to Karla Johnson for her brilliant ideas and guidance. Her support of ABT's efforts to make healthy training a national initiative is genuinely appreciated.

EDITORS:
Gary I. Wadler, MD, FACP, FACSM, FACPM, FCP (Chairman, ABT Medical Advisory Board)
Kate Lydon (Chief Editor)
Abigail Rasminsky (Associate Editor)
Kathryn Holmes (Copy Editor)

PHOTOGRAPHERS:
Erin Baiano (All photos in the text; back inside cover; and Part 2 cover page photos)
Rosalie O'Connor (All cover photos except for dancer in attitude; front inside cover; and Part 3 cover page photo)
Jerry Ruotolo (Cover photo of dancer in attitude)

DESIGNER:
Salvatore Garguilo

ILLUSTRATOR:
Thom Graves Media

Published by Macfadden Performing Arts Media

This handbook provides an outline of sample practices and represents a composite of views of the medical and dance professionals who have contributed to its preparation. However, this handbook is not meant to be, nor should it be, used by the reader in lieu of seeking and obtaining professional medical advice. Teachers, dancers, parents and other users of this handbook are advised to always seek professional counsel for their health and medical concerns. In addition, none of ABT, its affiliates, staff, trustees, teachers, administrators or contributors to this handbook, shall be responsible for any injury sustained or damage incurred as a direct or indirect result of participation in a program affiliated with the ABT Curriculum.

ISBN: 978-0-615-22779-5

Introduction

Since its founding in 1940, American Ballet Theatre has developed a reputation as one of the world's great ballet companies. Performing to more than 600,000 people annually, ABT regularly tours the United States and has danced in more than 43 countries. In recognition of its cultural contributions and extensive outreach, the United States Congress formally recognized ABT as America's National Ballet Company in 2006.

As a national ballet company, ABT understands that it has a responsibility to take a leadership role in dance training and dance education in the United States. Through conversations with ABT's artistic faculty and dance teachers across America, it became clear that a comprehensive resource was needed to address the whole dancer—including the basics of dancer health and child development for all ages and skill levels.

To that end, ABT assembled a Medical Advisory Board to provide guidelines for the healthy and sound training of dancers. The advisory board, headed by Gary I. Wadler, MD, FACP, FACSM, FACPM, FCP, includes world-renowned medical professionals from the fields of sports medicine, nutrition, physical therapy and orthopedics. The panel gathered to discuss the most prevalent topics in dance training today. Subcommittees in orthopedics and injury prevention, health and wellness, and facility standards also provide recommendations for teachers that can be used to enhance an already existing curriculum.

It is our hope that *The Healthy Dancer: ABT Guidelines for Dancer Health* will positively impact the training of young dancers in America. Thank you for joining us in this effort.

Kevin McKenzie
Artistic Director
American Ballet Theatre

Rachel S. Moore
Executive Director
American Ballet Theatre

Preface

In recent years, there has been a remarkable growth in the number of ballet schools throughout the United States. However, the competency of those teaching this physically and mentally challenging art form may not have grown commensurately. Too often, dance instructors lack the requisite knowledge, at least with respect to the health and safety of their students.

In 2006, the United States Congress passed a resolution designating American Ballet Theatre, with its 65 years of experience, as America's National Ballet Company. In doing so, the Congress recognized "that the American Ballet Theatre's extensive and innovative education, outreach and artistic development programs both train future generations of great dancers and expose students to the arts."

With that resolution came a responsibility to bring "innovative education and outreach" to ballet schools throughout America.

Accordingly, at the behest of Lewis Ranieri, Chairman Emeritus of the Board of the American Ballet Theatre, and with the insightful help of its Executive Director, Rachel Moore, its Artistic Director, Kevin McKenzie, and their staff, and the assistance of the American College of Sports Medicine, the American Ballet Theatre Medical Advisory Board was established. This diverse group of experts in dance medicine and sports medicine, representing some of the best minds in the country and countless years of experience, met to address the challenge of creating comprehensive state-of-the-art health and medical guidelines for ballet instruction and establishing the best practices relative to dance pedagogy.

The curriculum that follows is not about the artistry of dance, but rather it is a unique resource about the health, medical and psychological underpinnings of ballet that should, indeed must, be integrated into the curricula of ballet schools throughout the United States. Its focus is not on the professional dancer, but rather on young dancers, pre-professional dancers and recreational dancers.

By incorporating the guidelines that follow into school curricula, teachers can ensure that dance in America continues to evolve and mature as a safe and sound physical art form.

Gary I. Wadler, MD, FACP, FACSM, FACPM, FCP
Chairman
Medical Advisory Board
American Ballet Theatre

The ABT Medical Advisory Board

Gary I. Wadler, MD (Chairman)
Clinical Associate Professor of Medicine
NYU School of Medicine

Phillip A. Bauman, MD
Assistant Clinical Professor
Orthopedic Surgery
College of Physicians and Surgeons
Columbia University

Lisa R. Callahan, MD
Associate Professor of Clinical Medicine
Weill Medical College of Cornell University

Priscilla M. Clarkson, PhD
Associate Dean for Research
School of Public Health & Health Sciences
University of Massachusetts

Julie Daugherty, MPT
ABT Physical Therapist

Franco De Vita
Principal, Jacqueline Kennedy Onassis School at ABT

Randall W. Dick
Associate Director of Research/Injury Surveillance System
NCAA

Christa Dickey
Director of Communications
American College of Sports Medicine

James G. Garrick, MD
Clinical Professor of Orthopedics
Department of Pediatrics
University of California, San Francisco

William Garnett Hamilton, MD
Clinical Professor of Orthopedic Surgery
College of Physicians and Surgeons
Columbia University

Raymond Lukens
Faculty, Jacqueline Kennedy Onassis School at ABT

Peter Marshall, MA, PT
ABT Physical Therapist

Kevin McKenzie
ABT Artistic Director

Lyle J. Micheli, MD
Assistant Clinical Professor of Orthopedic Surgery
Harvard Medical School

Rachel Moore, MA
ABT Executive Director

Lewis S. Ranieri
ABT Chairman Emeritus

Caroline Silby, PhD, MEd
Sports Psychologist
Adjunct Faculty
American University

Eric Small, MD
Assistant Clinical Professor of Pediatrics, Orthopedics and Rehabilitation Medicine
Mount Sinai School of Medicine

Angela D. Smith MD
Clinical Associate in Orthopedic Surgery
The Children's Hospital of Philadelphia
Department of Orthopedic Surgery

Virginia Wilmerding, PhD
Former President, International Association of Dance Medicine and Science
Adjunct Professor
University of New Mexico

Biographies on page 119

TABLE OF CONTENTS

CHAPTER 12: Nutrition 79

CHAPTER 13: Principles of Training 84

Health: Part 1

ANATOMY AND INJURIES

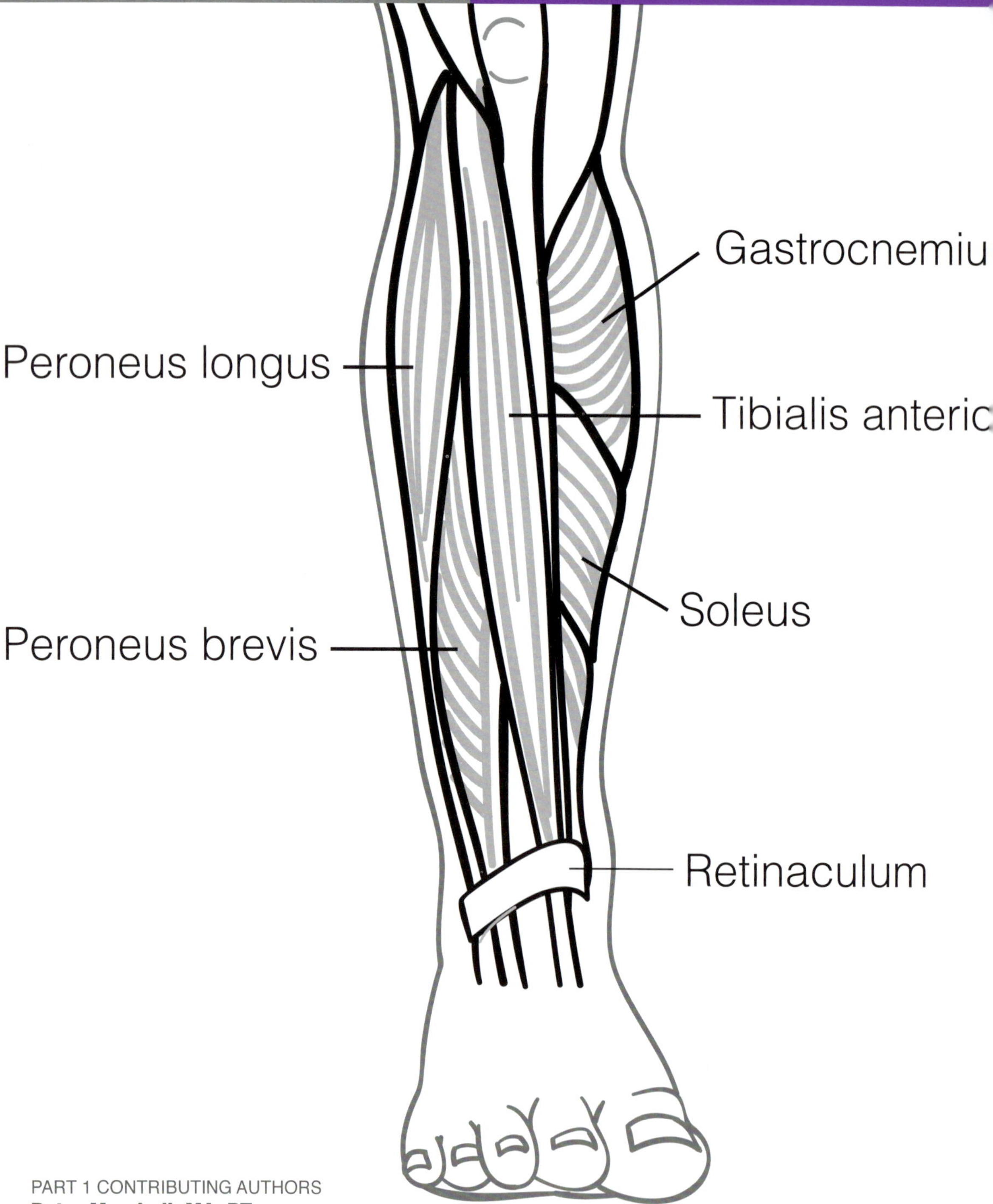

Gastrocnemiu

Peroneus longus

Tibialis anteric

Soleus

Peroneus brevis

Retinaculum

PART 1 CONTRIBUTING AUTHORS
Peter Marshall, MA, PT
William G. Hamilton, MD, BSE, AAOS, FACS
Phillip A. Bauman, MD
Julie Daugherty, MPT
James G. Garrick, MD
Angela D. Smith, MD

CHAPTER 1: Anatomy and Kinesiology

INTRODUCTION

In order to understand the human body and how it moves, and to prevent and heal injuries, it is important that we have some knowledge of human anatomy. The body has often been likened to a machine, and like a machine, it has physical limitations. It can break down or wear out, and it is critical that we understand those limits if we wish to protect it.

This chapter is not meant to be an all-inclusive description of human anatomy and function. It is meant instead to introduce certain concepts that will allow a better understanding of the underlying structure (anatomy) of the body and how the various parts of the machine work together to allow dancers to move.

Our bodies are made of living cells. Most of these cells, visible only under a microscope, have quite specialized functions and perform different operations. For example, our brains are composed of nerve cells that are connected together physically, electrically and chemically to allow signals to be sent and received from all over the body.

The musculoskeletal system is comprised of bones, muscles, ligaments and tendons. It protects our internal organs (such as our brain, heart, lungs, kidneys, liver and intestines) and provides our bodies with internal and external support. The two main organs of the musculoskeletal system are muscles and bones.

Muscles are comprised of many small cells that work together to move the body. The pulling force generated by our muscles is referred to as "tension" and is the same physical term that we use in describing the tightness of a rope.

There are two types of energy production that fuel our muscles: aerobic and anaerobic metabolism. Aerobic metabolism depends on the blood stream to deliver oxygen to the muscles for fuel, whereas anaerobic metabolism supplies fuel to the working muscles in the absence of oxygen. Endurance activities are primarily dependent upon the aerobic system, and activities that are of high intensity and short duration primarily depend on the anaerobic system.

Bones are the other main part of the musculoskeletal system. They comprise the skeleton of the body.

Other anatomical structures in this system are the tendons, ligaments and cartilage.

Tendons are the strings or cords that attach muscles to bones. One well-known tendon is the Achilles tendon (in the back of the ankle). [See FIGURE 1.] The Achilles tendon connects the calf muscle (gastrocnemius) to the back of the heel (calcaneus) bone. When the calf muscle contracts and tightens, the tension is transmitted to the heel bone via the Achilles tendon. If the tension is great enough, the calf and the Achilles tendon tighten to pull the heel toward the back of the knee, permitting us to walk and ballet dancers to relevé. While there are several other muscles that perform a similar function around the ankle joint, the gastrocnemius muscle and Achilles tendon form the strongest muscle and tendon combination that permits us to point our feet at the ankles.

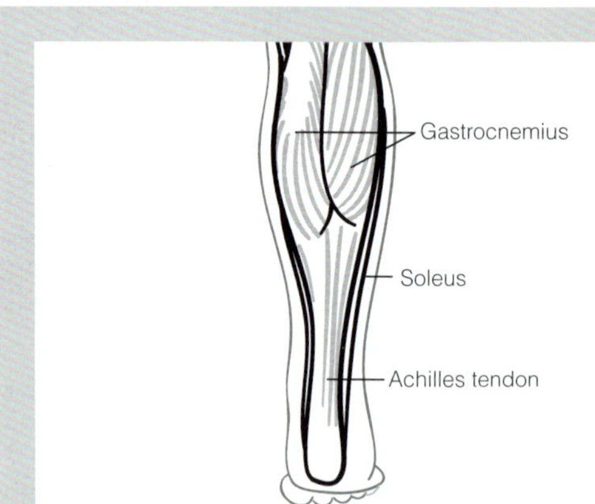

FIGURE 1. Muscles of the Right Lower Leg (Rear View).

Ligaments attach bones to each other and provide support to the skeleton. [See FIGURE 2.] They are sometimes referred to as "static stabilizers" because they don't contract or shorten.

Working together, the bones, muscles, ligaments and tendons allow the dancer to move.

BONES, MUSCLES, LIGAMENTS AND TENDONS

BONES

Description: There are approximately 206 bones in the human body. Occasionally extra (accessory) bones may be present, most commonly in the hands and feet. Bones are made of a hard, outer part called the cortex, and a softer inner part called cancellous bone (which contains the bone marrow). The hard, outer cortex provides much of the strength of any bone.

Functions:

- **To provide structural support for the body:** Bones stabilize the body and provide scaffolding.
- **To protect the organs:** Bones form a solid protective "wall" around many of the critical organs in our body. The most solidly protected organ, the brain, is surrounded by a series of bones (the skull) that are joined together by non-moveable joints. The ribcage forms a protective barrier for the organs within the chest cavity—including the lungs, heart and major vessels in the body, an artery called the aorta and a vein called the vena cava. The ribcage cannot be as solid as the skull, because it must permit motion to allow the lungs to expand and contract so that we may breathe. This expansion

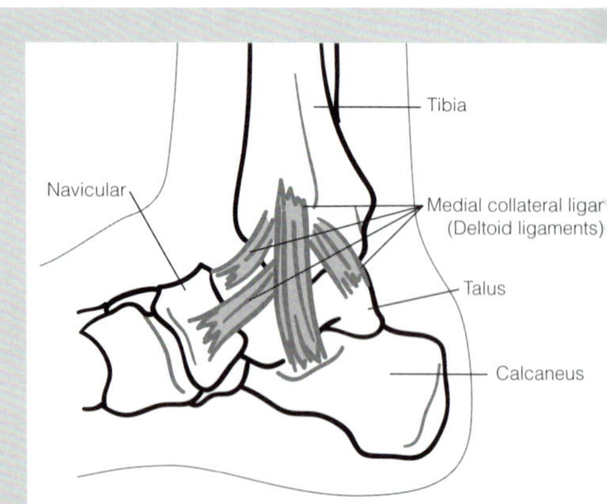

FIGURE 2. Medial Ankle Ligaments (Right Ankle, Medial View)

and contraction occurs at joints that connect the ribs to bones of the thoracic spine (thoracic vertebrae) and joints that connect ribs to a solid bone at the front of the ribcage, called the sternum.

- **To produce blood:** Blood cells are formed within the cancellous portion (bone marrow) of some bones, including the pelvis and the ribs. The cancellous portion of the bone is softer, less dense and populated with many different types of cells including those that produce red blood cells.
- **To allow growth:** Growing bones have an area of growth at the end of the bone that is comprised of cartilage cells, called the epiphysis, or growth plate. [See FIGURE 3.] During periods of rapid growth, the epiphysis widens and is weaker than the surrounding bone and is easily injured.
- **To store calcium:** Most of the calcium that we store in our bones is added during childhood and adolescence. Once we reach adulthood, our calcium stores cannot be as significantly increased, so it is critical that we have adequate calcium in our diet when we are growing.

Types of Bones:

- **Long (tubular):** Femur, tibia, humerus, radius, ulna
- **Flat:** Pelvis, ribs, cranium (skull)
- **Sesamoids:** Two small bones encased in tendons (similar to miniature kneecaps) that lie under the head of the 1st metatarsal bone in the ball of the foot just beneath the big toe joint itself. [See FIGURE 4.]

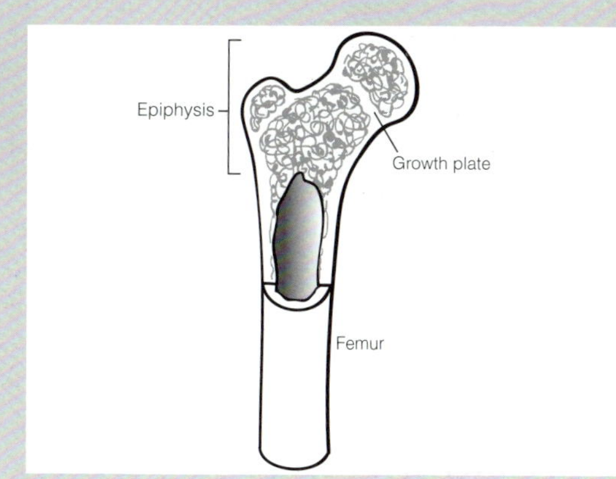

FIGURE 3. Epiphysis

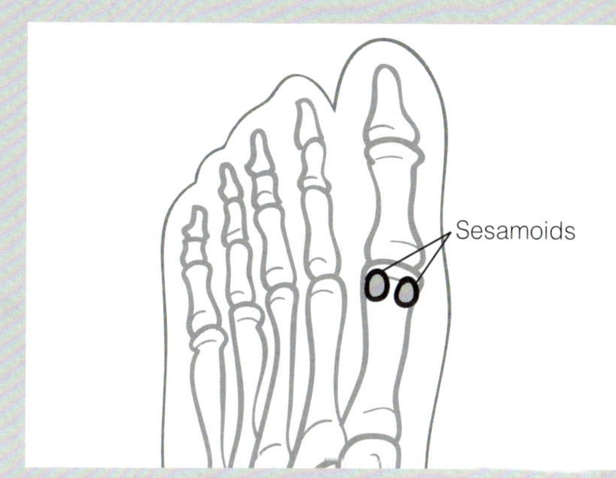

FIGURE 4. Sesamoid Bones (Right Foot, View from Below)

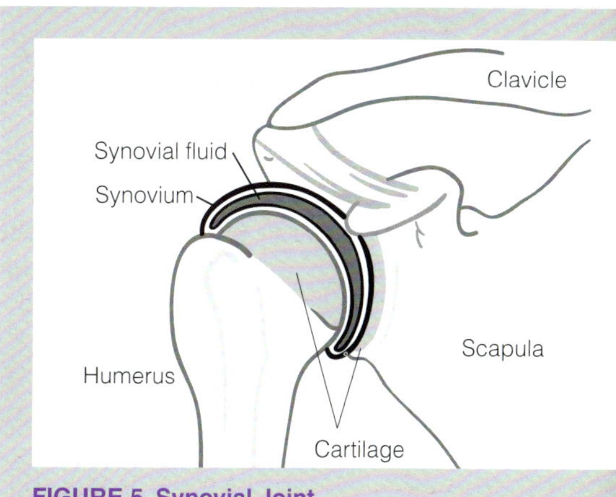

FIGURE 5. Synovial Joint (Right Shoulder, Front View)

JOINTS

Description: Joints form the connections between bones. There are several types of joints. Some are quite limited in movement, while others allow a considerable amount.

Functions:

- To provide movement
- To join bones together

Types of Joints:

Synovial joint: The most common type of joint and the type that allows the most motion is called a synovial joint. [See FIGURE 5.] Synovial joints are surrounded by a capsule, which is made of a layer of fibrous connective tissue. The bone surfaces within all synovial joints are covered with a smooth layer of cartilage called articular or hyaline cartilage. Articular cartilage is nourished and lubricated by synovial fluid, which is produced by the lining of the capsule called the synovium. The largest and most commonly injured synovial joints in the extremities fall into one of three types:

- **Ball and socket:** The shoulders and the hips are ball and socket joints. These allow motion in several different planes, as well as rotation. [See FIGURES 5 and 6.]
- **Hinge:** The main part of the elbow is a hinge joint, which permits movement principally in one plane. [See FIGURE 7.]
- **Modified hinge:** The ankles and knees may be thought of as modified hinge joints because motion in the joint is not strictly limited to one plane. [See FIGURE 8.]

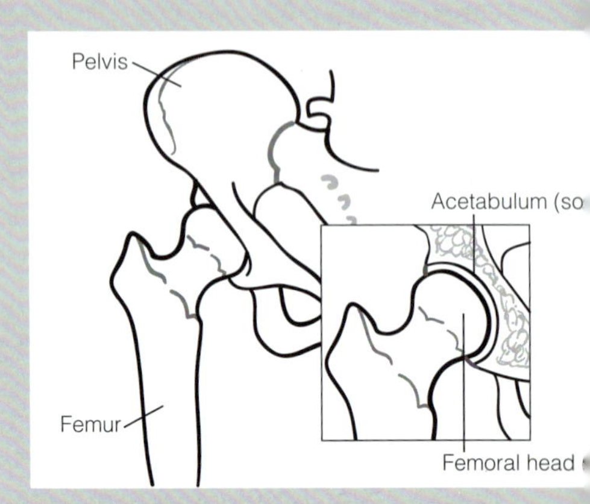

FIGURE 6. Ball and Socket Joint (Right Hip, Front View)

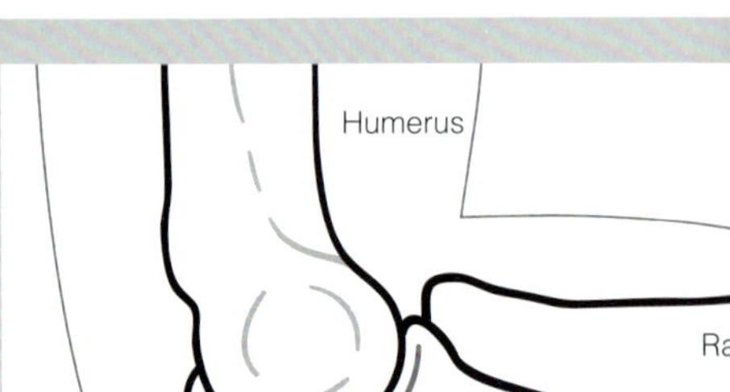

FIGURE 7. Hinge Joint (Left Elbow, Medial View)

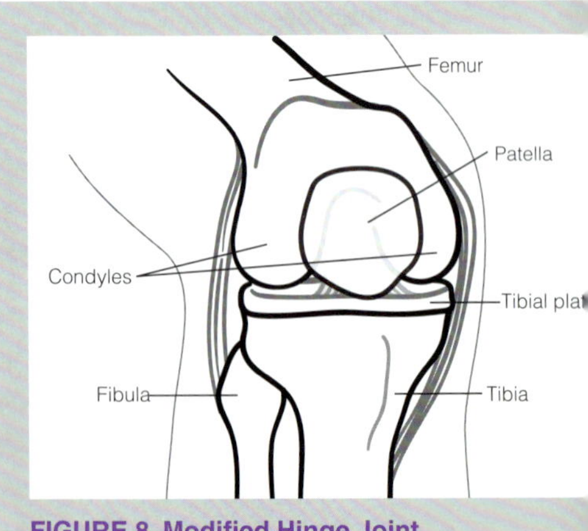

FIGURE 8. Modified Hinge Joint (Right Knee, Front View)

Fibrous joint: These joints connect bones and allow for little or no motion. Examples include a syndesmosis, such as between the tibia and fibula at the top of the ankle joint. In a syndesmosis, two bones are separated by a larger space, but united by fibrous connective tissue (like a ligament). [See FIGURE 9.]

Cartilaginous joint: These are united by hyaline cartilage and allow for only a little movement. There are two sub-types: a symphysis and a synchondrosis. The most important examples of symphysis joints are the unions between the vertebral bodies—they are joined together by a heavy fibrous intervertebral disc, which allows bending motion between individual vertebrae—and the pubic symphysis in the pelvis, which joins the front left and right pubic bones together. [See FIGURES 10 and 11.] Most synchondroses, such as the joints connecting the ribs to the sternum, or breastbone, disappear upon full development of the skeleton.

LIGAMENTS

Description: Ligaments are the structures that hold joints together. They connect bone to bone and allow motion only in certain directions. They are made of dense connective tissue and are only slightly elastic. An injury to a ligament is called a sprain.

Function: Ligaments provide primary support for joints.

MUSCLES

Description: Muscles are the motors that allow the body to move parts of the body relative to other parts. The muscle type responsible for moving extremities and external areas of the body is called "skeletal muscle."

Function: Muscles are a source of power.

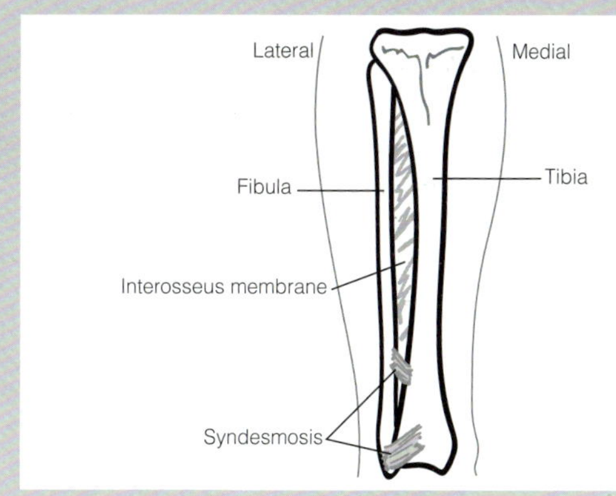

FIGURE 9. Syndesmosis (Right Leg, Front View)

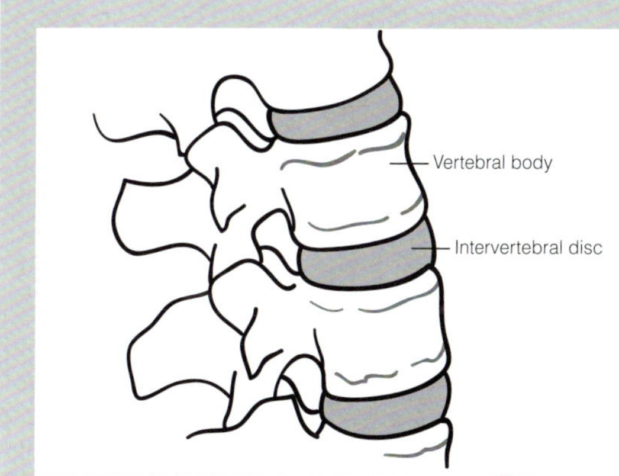

FIGURE 10. Cartilaginous Joint (Lumbar Spine)

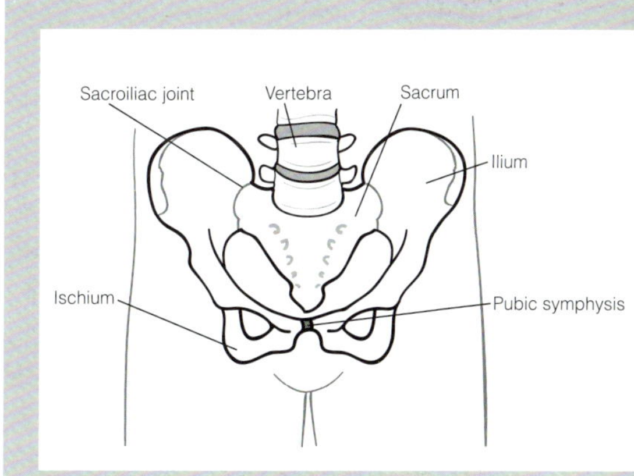

FIGURE 11. Pelvis

TENDONS

Description: Tendons are the strings or cords that connect muscles to bones. They are surrounded by a tendon sheath through which the tendon travels. Some tendons travel through fibrous and bony tunnels around various joints. An injury to a tendon or a muscle is called a strain.

Function: Tendons transfer force from the muscle to the bone to produce the movements of the joints.

PARTS OF THE BODY

ANKLE

Function: The ankle is a modified hinge joint. Motion of the ankle joint includes dorsiflexion and plantar flexion (flexing and pointing, respectively). [See FIGURE 12.] The ankle also allows eversion and inversion, a side-to-side motion that helps the foot accommodate to uneven surfaces. [See FIGURE 13.]

Description: The ankle includes the true ankle joint and the subtalar joint which lies beneath it. [See FIGURE 14.] The true ankle joint is responsible for up and down motion of the foot, whereas the subtalar joint (between the talus and calcaneus, or heel bone) allows side-to-side motion of the heel, which allows the foot to turn in and out (inversion and eversion). The large bony prominences on the inner (medial) and outer (lateral) sides of the ankle are referred to as the malleoli (singular = malleolus). The inner (medial) malleolus is part of the far end of the tibia. It extends down to partially overlap and articulate with the talus bone. The outer (lateral) malleolus is a portion of a parallel bone, the fibula. The two bones, tibia (medial malleolus) and fibula (lateral malleolus), are positioned in a way that stabilizes the talus and prevents it from moving out of place or dislocating to the side. The talus lies between these two bones in the "mortise" of the ankle joint.

Ligaments: The ligaments of the ankle are grouped into two categories, the lateral collateral ligaments and medial collateral (deltoid) ligaments. [See FIGURES 2 and 15.] Although the ligaments of the ankle are strong fibrous bands, they are often susceptible to injury. The tibia and fibula are joined,

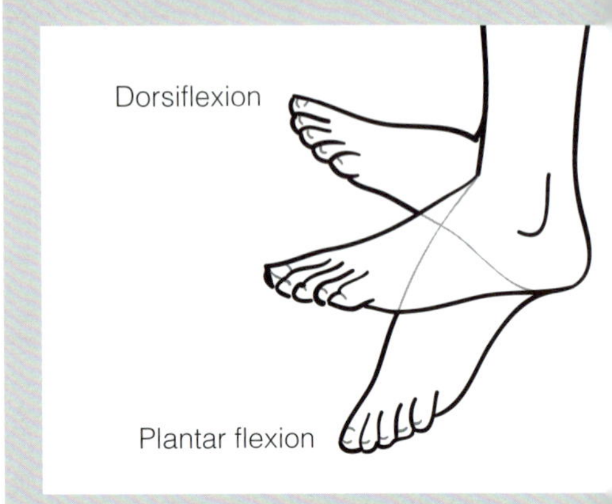

FIGURE 12. Foot Flexion

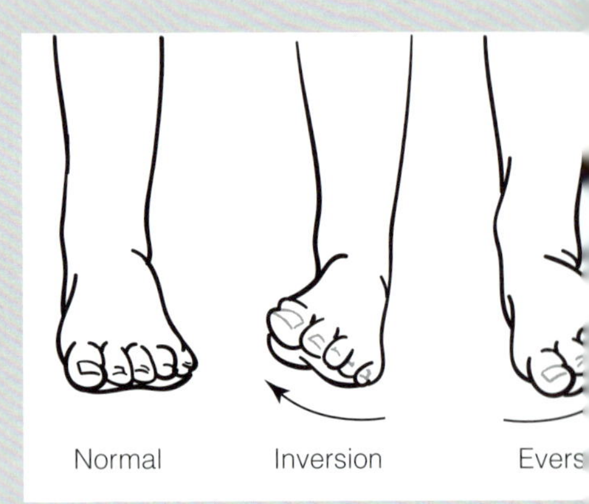

FIGURE 13. Foot Inversion and Eversion.

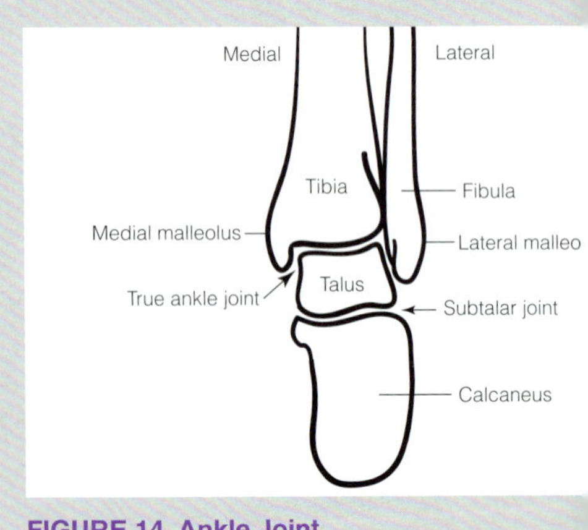

FIGURE 14. Ankle Joint (Right Ankle, Rear View).

just above the ankle, by several ligaments which help support and stabilize the joint. [See FIGURE 9.] These ligaments are called the tibio-fibular ligaments and include the inferiorly located syndesmosis. Injury to the syndesmosis is referred to as a high ankle sprain. Injury of the lateral (or outer) ligaments of the ankle is the most common type of ankle sprain.

Muscles and Tendons:

- **Peroneal Muscles and Tendons:** The peroneal muscles and tendons course along the outer (lateral) aspect of the ankle and foot. These muscles control a dancer's ability to wing the foot. [See PHOTO 1; FIGURE 16.]
- **Posterior Tibial Muscle and Tendon:** The posterior tibialis, which courses along the back of the ankle and foot, controls the ability to sickle the foot. It attaches principally to the navicular bone but has other attachments in the same area. [See PHOTO 1; FIGURE 17.]
- **Achilles Tendon:** The Achilles tendon is the largest tendon in the body and connects the large calf muscles—the gastrocnemius muscles and the soleus—to the heel bone (calcaneus). [See FIGURE 1.]

ELBOW

Function: The elbow is principally a hinge joint that permits straightening (extension) and bending (flexion) between the upper arm and forearm. [See FIGURE 7.]

Description: The movement of the elbow involves three bones: the humerus, the ulna and the radius. The humerus and ulna come together to form a very tight hinge joint allowing motion in one plane (extension and flexion). The radius articulates within the joint, permitting rotation of the forearm—pronation (palms down) and supination (palms up).

Muscles: Two of the more important muscle groups are the biceps and triceps for flexion and extension of the elbow, respectively. Other important muscles that effect movement of the elbow are the brachialis and the brachioradialis. [See FIGURE 18.]

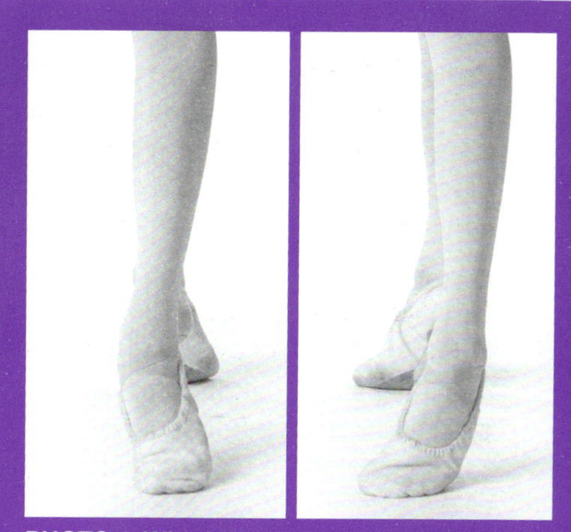

PHOTO 1. Winging and Sickling

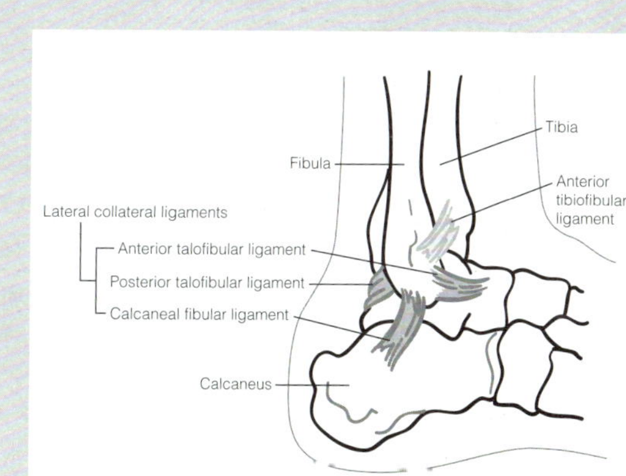

FIGURE 15 Lateral Ankle Ligaments (Right Ankle, Side View)

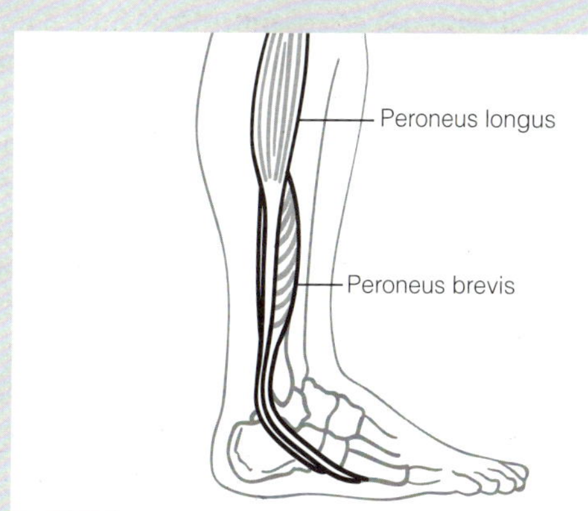

FIGURE 16. Peroneus Muscles (Right Leg, Lateral View)

FOOT

Function: The foot is an extremely complex anatomic structure made up of 26 bones and 33 joints that work together with 107 ligaments, muscles and tendons to execute precise movements. [See FIGURE 19.]

Description: The foot is divided into three parts: the hind foot, mid foot and fore foot. The five long bones in the fore foot are called the metatarsals. The heaviest, strongest metatarsal is the first metatarsal, which runs from the first cuneiform bone of the foot to the base of the big toe. The second through fifth, or lesser, metatarsals are much thinner in diameter and therefore subject to stress injury or fracture.

(See page 15 for Toes.)

HIP

Function: The hip joint is a strong ball and socket joint and is one of the most secure joints in the body. Its primary function is to support the weight of the body while standing, walking, running or dancing.

Description: The hip joint is formed by the socket (acetabulum), located in the pelvis, and the ball of the femur (femoral head). The hip joint is typically a deeper ball and socket joint than the shoulder joint, and is quite stable. It is rimmed by cartilage called the acetabular labrum, which can tear (see Injuries Listed By Body Part, Hip). [See FIGURE 20.]

Ligaments: The hip has strong ligaments, which are thickenings in the joint capsule called iliofemoral ligaments. [See FIGURE 21.] The iliofemoral ligaments tend to be tighter when the hip is straight (extended); it is therefore easier to externally rotate, or turn out at the hip, when the hip is flexed, for instance in plié. Turnout is also easier, although not correct, when the lower back is swayed in a lordotic position. A swayed back allows the pelvis to flex relative to the thigh, or femur. (See Chapter Four for more on turnout.)

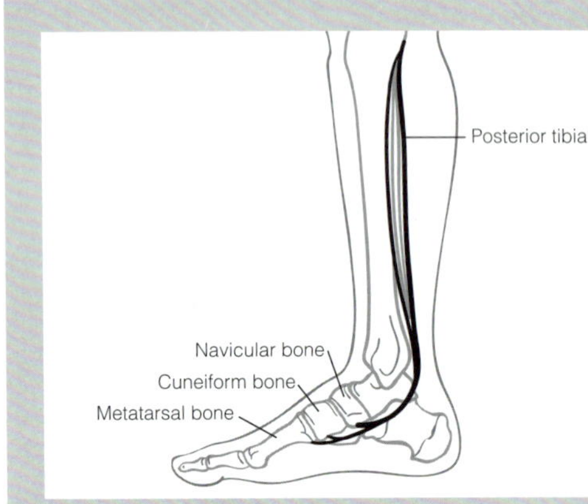

FIGURE 17. Posterior Tibial Muscle (Right Leg, Medial View)

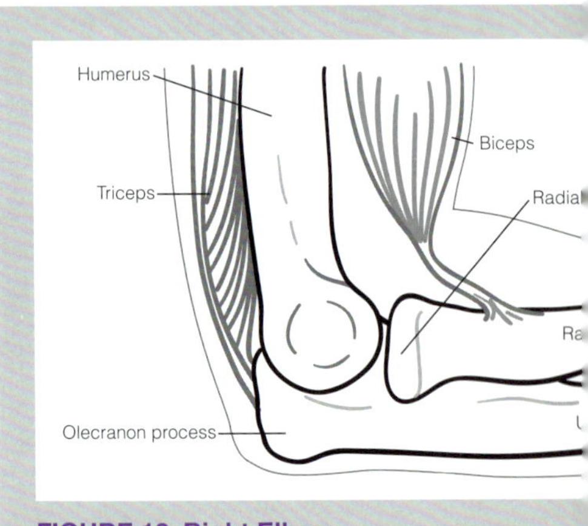

FIGURE 18. Right Elbow (Lateral View)

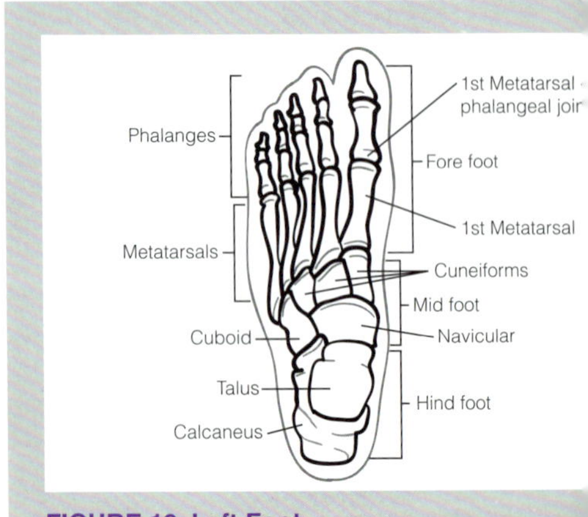

FIGURE 19. Left Foot (Top View)

Muscles:

- **Iliopsoas:** The strongest muscle in the body, the iliopsoas stretches across the hip joint and flexes the hip and thigh in the forward plane (such as in developpé front). [See FIGURE 22.]

- **Internal and external rotators:** Other muscles around the hip include the internal and external rotators (similar to those found in the shoulder) that control turnout and turn in, the abductors that allow the leg to rise laterally (to the side), and the adductors that allow movement toward the midline of the body.

- **Quadriceps:** The quadriceps muscle is in the front of the thigh. It enables bending (flexion) of the hip and straightening (extension) of the knee (as in developpé front). Tightness in the quads may limit the ability to bend, or flex, the knee fully. [See FIGURE 23.]

- **Hamstrings:** The hamstrings are in the back of the thigh. They control flexion of the knee and assist in extension of the hip (as in arabesque). Tightness in the hamstrings may prevent full flexion of the hip and full extension of the knee. [See FIGURE 24.].

Note: External rotation, or turnout of the hip, is controlled by strong external rotator muscles in the buttocks. The bony configuration of the socket, head and neck of the femur, which cannot be altered, determines a dancer's range of turnout.

(See page 13 for Pelvis.)

KNEE

Function: The knee is a modified hinge joint because it allows for some rotation as well as flexion and extension. [See FIGURE 8.]

Description: The knee joint is formed by the femur above, the tibia below and the patella (kneecap) in front. The quadriceps tendon attaches to the top of the patella, and the patellar tendon runs from the bottom of the patella down to the tibia attaching to a specific prominent portion of the tibia called the tibial

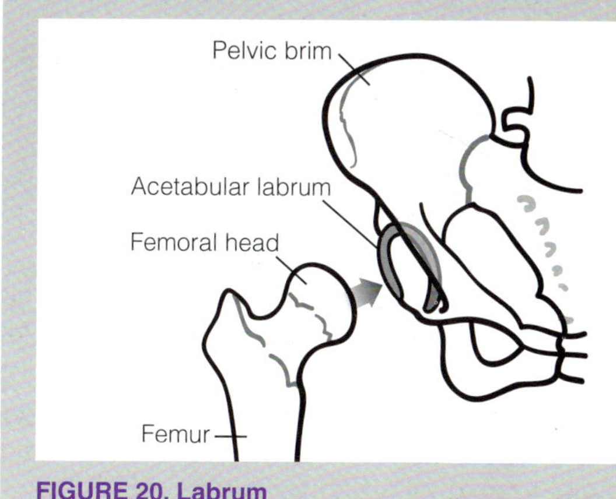

FIGURE 20. Labrum (Right Hip, Front View)

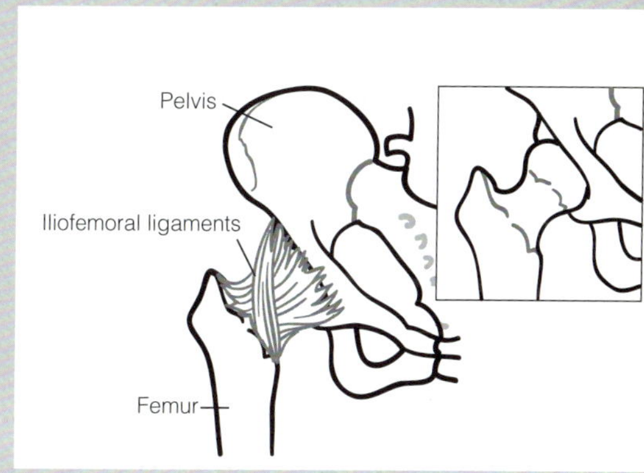

FIGURE 21. Iliofemoral Ligaments (Right Hip, Front View)

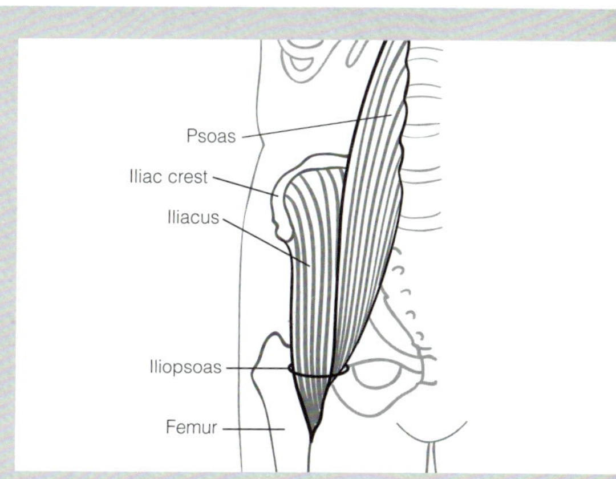

FIGURE 22. Iliopsoas Muscle (Right, Front View)

tubercle. [See FIGURE 25.] The patella glides on the front surface of the femur and should sit centered in a groove on the femur called the trochlea.

The femoral condyles sit within the knee joint and rest upon the top part of the tibia, called the tibial plateau. The relatively flat tibial plateau permits the femur to move forward and back relative to the tibia, in addition to some twisting, or rotation, and flexion and extension.

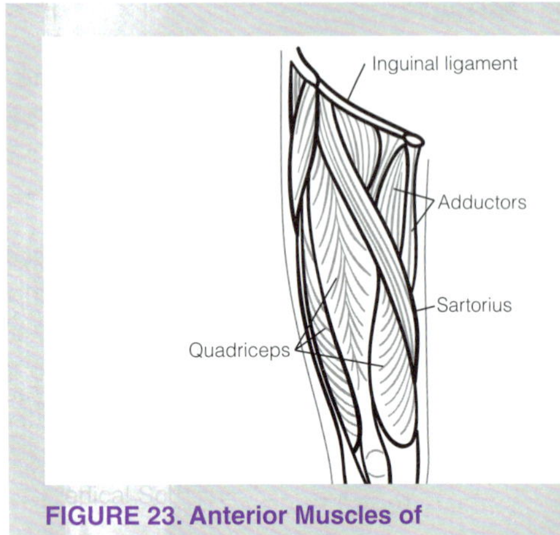

FIGURE 23. Anterior Muscles of Right Thigh (Front View)

Ligaments:

Several important ligaments support the knee:

- Medial and lateral collateral ligaments: The collateral ligaments prevent abnormal side-to-side motion of the knee.
- Anterior cruciate ligament (ACL): One of the two central ligaments within the knee joint, the anterior cruciate prevents hyperextension of the knee. Because it is attached obliquely from the femur to the tibia, it also helps to control rotation of the femur on the tibia.
- Posterior cruciate ligament: The posterior cruciate ligament similarly aids in controlling abnormal rotation.

[See FIGURE 26.]

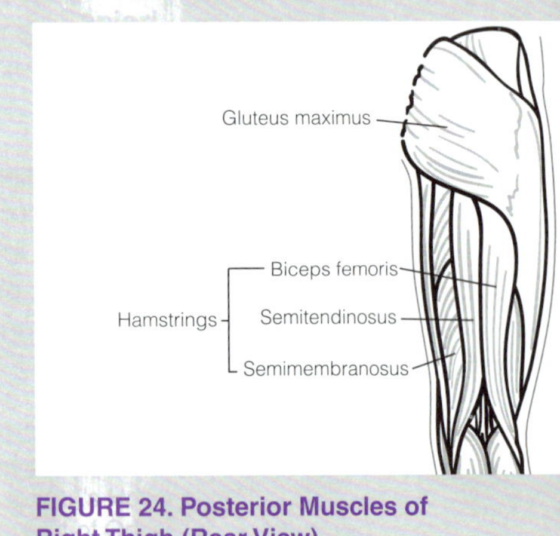

FIGURE 24. Posterior Muscles of Right Thigh (Rear View)

Muscles:

The muscles that act on the knee to cause extension are:

- The quadriceps, a group of four muscles—the vastus medialis, intermedialis and lateralis, and the rectus femorus. [See FIGURE 25.]

Flexors of the knee include:

- The hamstrings, which consist of three major muscles: the semitendinosus and the semimembranosus, which together make up the medial hamstring, and the biceps femoris, which is the lateral hamstring. [See FIGURE 24.]
- Additional flexors of the knee are the gracilis and sartorius muscles.

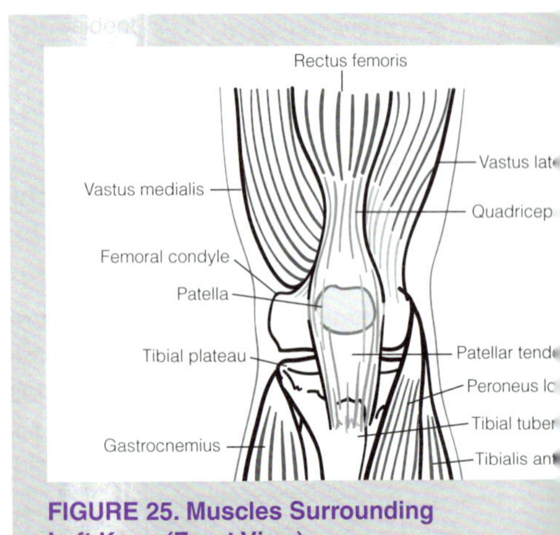

FIGURE 25. Muscles Surrounding Left Knee (Front View)

Additional muscles that originate or attach near and around the knee joint include:

- Popliteus and gastrocnemius, which attach, in part, to the back of the knee joint.

Menisci: Within the knee are two cartilaginous structures called the medial and lateral menisci (singular = meniscus). [See FIGURE 27.] These are attached to the edge of the knee joint and are sometimes called semi-lunar cartilages because they are shaped like half-moons. They help to cushion the knee joint, and they cradle the femoral condyles. They provide shock absorption and additional stability to the knee. The layman's expression "torn cartilage" generally refers to a tear in either the inner (medial) or outer (lateral) meniscus.

LOWER LEG, TIBIA AND FIBULA

Function: The bones of the lower leg provide structural stability.

Description: The bones of the lower leg are the larger tibia and the smaller fibula. These long, straight bones are analogous to the radius and the ulna in the forearm. [See FIGURE 9.]

Ligament: The tibia and fibula are connected to each other just above the ankle by a strong ligament called the syndesmosis (see page 6), which allows some limited motion between the two bones.

Muscles:

- **Anterior compartment muscles:** The muscles in the front of the lower leg are the anterior compartment muscles that move the foot upward. This is called dorsiflexion, but in ballet is usually referred to simply as flexion. The reciprocal motion (plantar flexion) is called pointing by dancers. [See FIGURE 28.]

- **Gastrocnemius and soleus muscles:** The muscles behind the tibia in the back of the lower leg include the strong gastrocnemius and soleus muscles (otherwise known as the calf muscles). These muscles (with the help of the Achilles tendon and the smaller toe flexor muscles) point (plantar flex) the foot and flex the toes. [See FIGURE 1.]

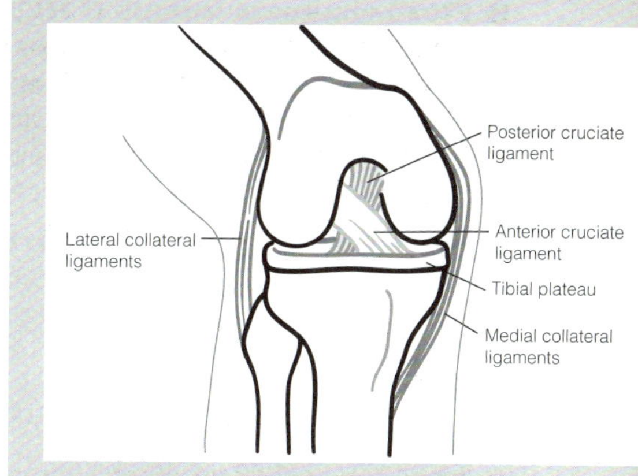

FIGURE 26. Ligaments of Right Knee (Front View)

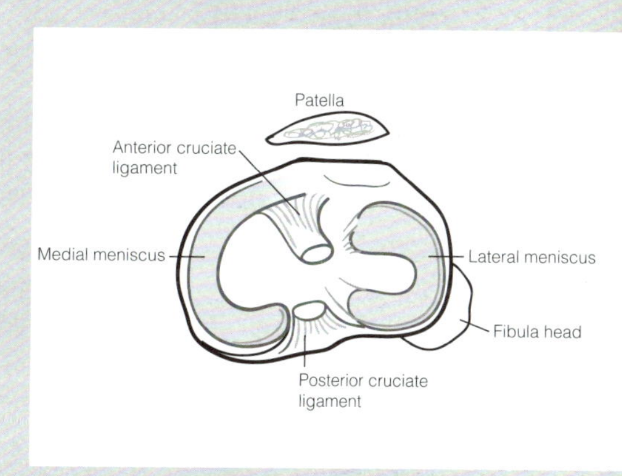

FIGURE 27. Menisci (Right Knee, From Above)

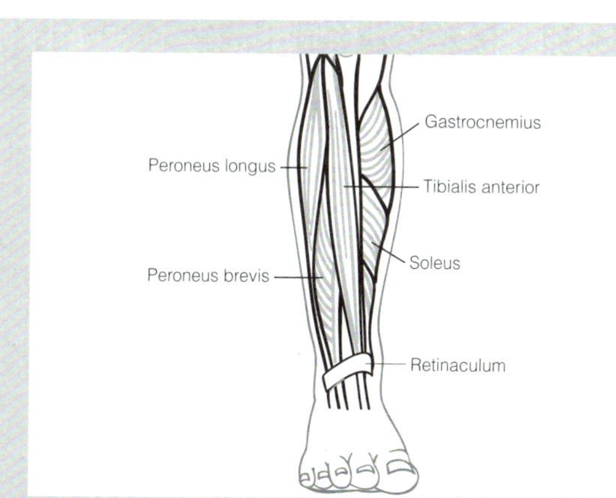

FIGURE 28. Muscles of Right Lower Leg (Front View)

- **Flexor hallucis longus (FHL):** The most important of the toe flexor muscles attaches to the big toe (great toe) and is called the flexor hallucis longus (FHL). This muscle is critical to a dancer's ability to fully point his or her foot. [See FIGURE 29.]
- **Peroneus longus, peroneus brevis:** The fourth group of muscles in the lower leg controls outward movement or winging of the foot. These are called the peroneal muscles—the longus and the brevis. Both are used to wing the foot outward and are important in stabilizing the foot, especially in demi- or full-pointe. [See PHOTO 1.] Strong peroneal muscles are the major protectors against ankle sprains. They run down the outside of the lower leg and along the outside of the ankle. [See FIGURE 16.]

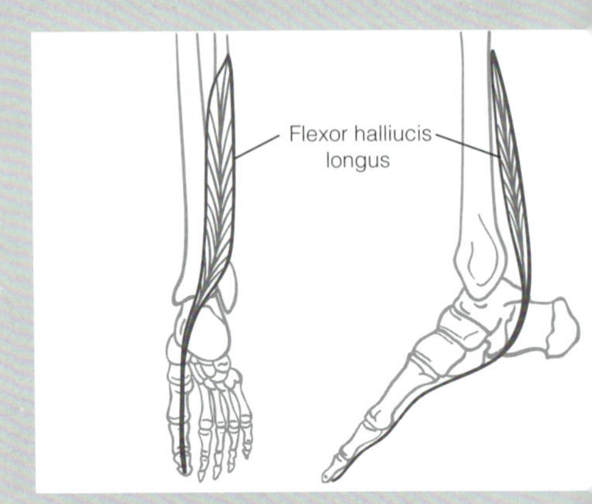

FIGURE 29. Flexor Hallucis Longus (Right Foot, Rear and Medial Views)

PELVIS

Function: In addition to protecting the reproductive organs and the bladder and bowels, the pelvis provides major structural support within the body.

Description: At the base of the spine, the pelvis forms a ring comprised of three distinct parts: the ilium, the pubis (in front) and the sacrum (in back). The sacroiliac joint, which joins the ilium and sacrum, is a strong, weight-bearing joint. [See FIGURE 30.]

(See page 9 for Hip.)

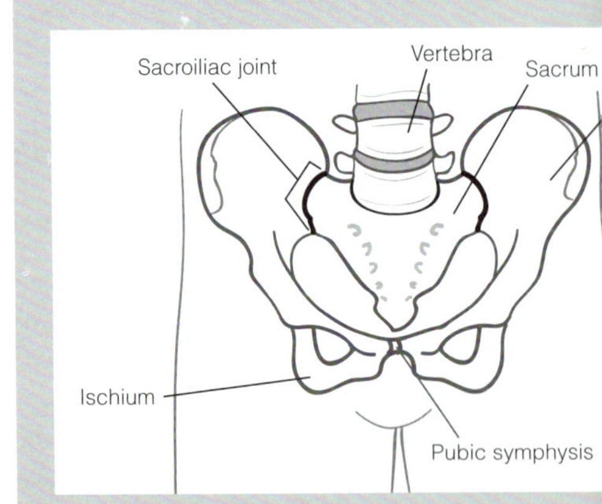

FIGURE 30. Sacroiliac Joints (Pelvis, Front View)

SHOULDER

Function: The shoulder is a shallow ball and socket joint that allows motion in several different planes, as well as rotation.

Description: The ball-like structure atop the upper arm bone (humerus), known as the humeral head, articulates with a shallow socket called the glenoid, which is a part of the shoulder blade (scapula). [See FIGURE 5.] The glenoid socket is rimmed by a type of cartilage called the glenoid labrum, which adds stability to the shoulder.

Shoulder motion occurs primarily through the glenoid and humeral head—the most mobile joint in the body—and additional motion is provided through movement of the scapula on the posterior chest wall. Up to one-third of overall shoulder movement may be due to movement between the scapula and the chest wall.

Ligaments: The shoulder joint has a variety of ligaments within the capsule of the joint, which help stabilize and support the joint.

Muscles: The surrounding muscles help provide substantial support and stability of the shoulder joint. Especially important are the rotator cuff muscles—a group of muscles that attach to the humeral head and enable shoulder rotation. [See FIGURE 31.] These muscles include one very strong internal rotator, the subscapularis, and three external rotators, the supraspinatus, infraspinatus and teres minor. All of the rotator cuff muscles attach to the humeral head at the greater or lesser tuberosity of the humerus. A tuberosity is a protuberance on a bone for attachment of a muscle or ligament.

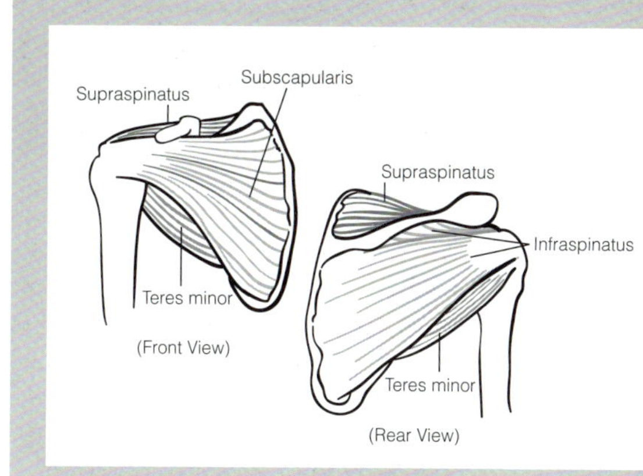

FIGURE 31. Rotator Cuff Muscles (Right Shoulder)

SPINE

Function: The spine forms the skeletal core of the torso and the axial support from which the body moves. It also protects the spinal cord. [See FIGURE 32.]

Description: The spine is comprised of multiple bones stacked on top of each other, called vertebrae. Vertebrae are connected by small synovial joints with a disc in between. [See FIGURE 10.]

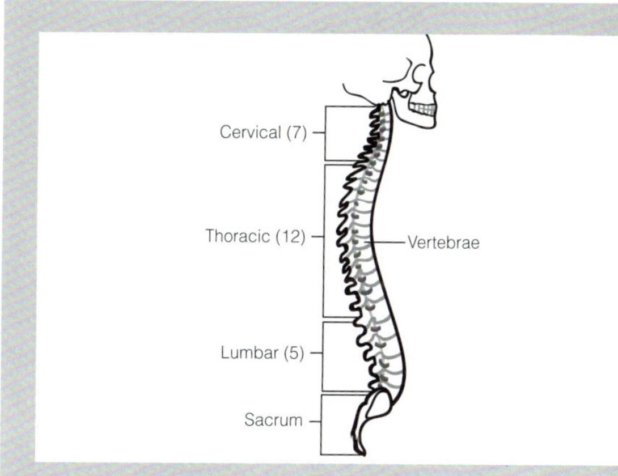

FIGURE 32. Spine

FOUR AREAS OF THE SPINAL COLUMN:

- **Cervical** (neck area): There are seven cervical vertebrae. Rotation in the cervical spine is provided through all of the vertebrae but especially through the first and second.
- **Thoracic** (chest and ribcage area): There are twelve thoracic vertebrae, each with a pair of ribs attached. The thoracic spine has much less motion than the cervical or lumbar spine due to the attachments of ribs to each vertebra.
- **Lumbar** (lower back area): There are five lumbar vertebrae. Most of the movement of the lower back occurs in the lumbar region.
- **Sacrum** (back of the pelvis): The sacrum is a single bone attached to the base of the spine, the coccyx and the hip bones.

Coccyx: There is a vestigial remnant called the coccyx—the so-called "tail-bone"—at the base of the spine. A vestigial remnant or organ is generally felt not to serve any significant function, although there are several ligaments between bones that attach to the coccyx. (Another example of a vestigial structure is the appendix.)

Intervertebral discs: The discs are fibrous structures with a firm outside ring of fibrous connective tissue and a soft, gelatinous center called the nucleus pulposus. [See FIGURE 33.] The discs are located in the neck (cervical), the mid-back (thoracic) and lower back (lumbar) and are responsible for one quarter of the entire length of the spine. They are considered semi-elastic structures and they lie between rigid vertebrae. They also act as shock absorbers when a vertical force or a sudden load is applied, like in jumping. Over time, their elasticity and resilience is lost.

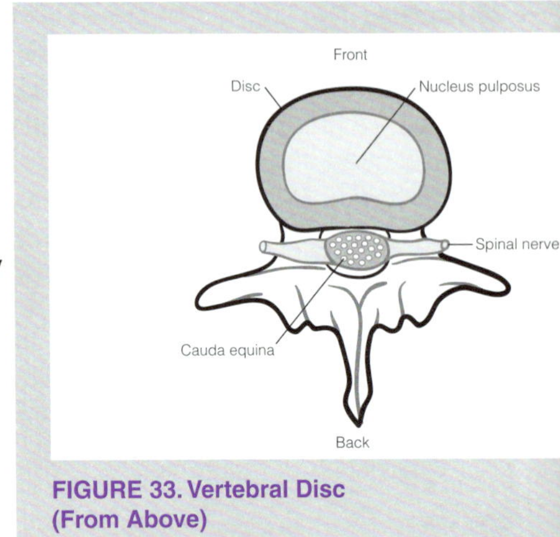

FIGURE 33. Vertebral Disc (From Above)

TOES

Description: The big toe joint—otherwise known as the first metatarsal-phalangeal joint (1st MPJ)—is a modified hinge joint. The joints of the four smaller toes (lesser metatarsal-phalangeal joints) are also modified hinge joints and are generally more flexible than the big toe joint (1st MPJ). The bones of the toes, like those of the fingers, are called phalanges (singular = phalanx). There are only two phalanges in the big toe; the four smaller toes generally have three small phalanges. [See FIGURE 19.]

Sesamoids: There are two small bones called sesamoids usually present underneath the big toe joint. Sesamoids are bones found within a tendon, near a joint (the kneecap or patella is another sesamoid bone). The two sesamoids under the big toe joint lie within one of the tendons of the flexor hallucis brevis muscle that assists with pointing the great toe. The four smaller toe joints lack sesamoid bones. [See FIGURE 4.]

Muscles and Tendon:

Flexor hallucis longus (FHL): The primary flexor of the big toe—critical to the dancer, especially with pointe work—is the flexor hallucis longus (FHL). The FHL is one of the deep muscles arising from the back of the leg and its tendon attaches to the undersurface of the base of the first toe. It works in concert with the flexor hallucis brevis muscle. [See FIGURE 29.]

CHAPTER 2: Dance-related Injuries and Common Medical Problems

INTRODUCTION

Ballet is generally a very safe and beneficial activity for young students. The vast majority of injuries can be attributed to attempts to achieve positions or movements that young bodies are either not suited for, or, in the environment of "extreme technique," exceed reasonable goals and/or expectations and intensity. It is important to recognize the physical limitations of each individual and tailor teaching requirements and expectations accordingly. By doing so, the dance teacher will decrease the potential for injury.

R.I.C.E.; Warning Signs of Injury; Fractures and Dislocations; Sprains and Strains

R.I.C.E.

For most mild (or even serious) injuries, applying **R.I.C.E.** treatments immediately will decrease pain, inflammation, muscle spasms, swelling and tissue damage. It achieves this by reducing blood flow to acutely injured tissues.

- **Rest:** Stop using the injured body part.
- **Ice:** Apply an ice pack to the injured area, using a towel or cover to protect your skin from frostbite. The more conforming the ice pack, the better. If an ice pack is not available, use a plastic bag of frozen peas or corn.
- **Compression:** Apply a pressure bandage or wrap over the ice pack to help reduce swelling. Never tighten the bandage or wrap to the point of cutting off blood flow.
- **Elevation:** The injured limb should be raised or propped up above the level of the heart.

WARNING SIGNS: IF AND WHEN A STUDENT NEEDS TO SEE A DOCTOR

The following signs may indicate to a teacher that a student is seriously injured and should be looked at by a health-care professional, preferably one with a background in dance:

- **Cannot bear weight normally:** Any time a dancer is not able to stand up and bear weight, there is a problem. If a dancer has fallen and can't get up and move normally after a few minutes, s/he has an acute injury that will need to be evaluated by a doctor as soon as possible. Immediately use R.I.C.E. on the injured area.
- **Experiencing pain or limping for more than two to three days:** Aches and pains are part of dancing, but healthy adolescents heal quickly and should recover from minor injuries rapidly. When they don't, they should be checked out medically, especially if the injured area is painful at night, making it hard for the dancer to sleep.

- **Cannot stand up straight and level:** To compensate for pain related to an injury, the dancer may assume an abnormal posture.
- **Has marked limitation or differences in motion of the joints of the back, hip, knee, ankle or foot:** The right and left sides of the body are not always equally strong or flexible. Minor differences in motion between the two sides can be normal, but a significant difference may indicate a problem.

FRACTURES AND DISLOCATIONS

- **In children and young adolescents:** Wrist and ankle injuries among children and young adolescents are rarely sprains. They are almost always fractures—often of the bone's growth plate (epiphysis)—because the ligaments are stronger than the growth plates. [See FIGURE 3.] Young dancers should promptly seek appropriate medical care after injuring a wrist or twisting an ankle, especially if there is swelling and inability to bear weight. In the interim, stop dancing and ice the area.
- **In older adolescents and adults:** Older adolescents may sustain ankle fractures through the growth plate that actually mimic ankle sprains with respect to swelling and apparent severity. Any dancer who cannot bear weight normally on his/her feet should have a prompt medical evaluation of the injury.

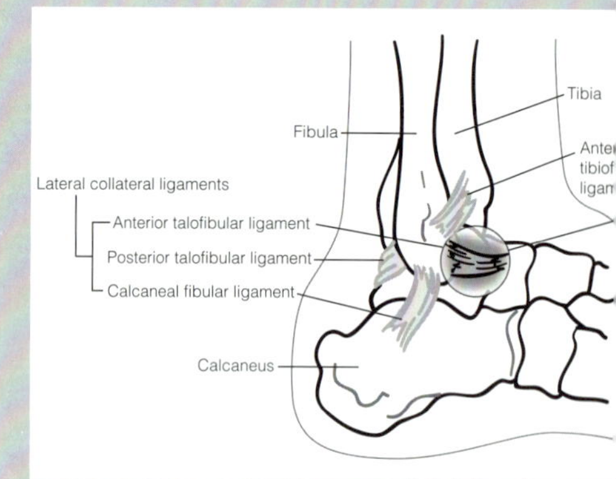

FIGURE 34. Sprain Lateral Ligament (Right Ankle, Side View)

- **When an arm or leg injury results in obvious deformity:** An untrained person should not attempt to correct the deformity, as further injury could occur. Help the dancer hold the injured limb still, or apply a splint in the position the limb is already in. Do not try to straighten the injured extremity, as this may cause further injury. Call an ambulance if the injury is severe. Immediate medical attention should be sought.
- **If there is no apparent deformity:** Use the R.I.C.E. principles. Make sure not to wrap an elastic bandage too tightly (the fingers or toes should have good color and not appear swollen). Using a splint, stirrup brace (for the ankle) or sling (for the arm) may help the dancer as s/he seeks medical attention. Dance schools should consider keeping splinting devices available in anticipation of such injuries.

SPRAINS AND STRAINS

A sprain is partial or complete tearing of a ligament, the structure that connects two bones. [See FIGURE 34.] A strain is partial or (rarely) complete tearing of a muscle-tendon structure, such as a complete tear of a hamstring. [See FIGURE 35.]

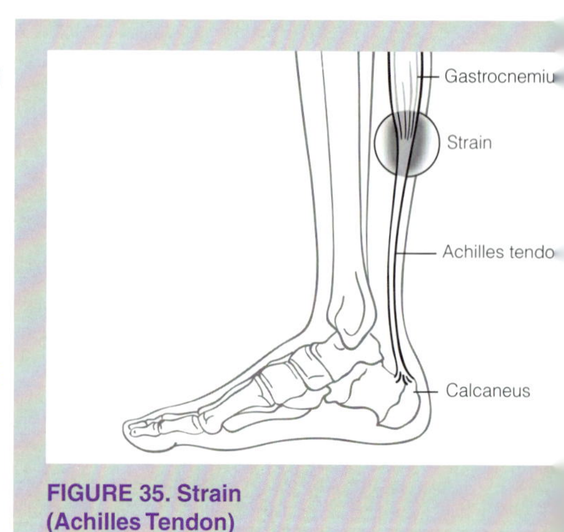

FIGURE 35. Strain (Achilles Tendon)

Implement the R.I.C.E. principles immediately if the dancer has sustained a sprain or a strain. Pain (especially when weight-bearing), swelling and discoloration are all good indicators as to the extent of the injury. A physician or physical therapist—preferably one with experience in dance medicine—should evaluate any sprain or strain immediately. The physician will be able to evaluate the extent of the injury and establish a treatment plan.

INJURIES LISTED BY BODY PART

ANKLE

Accessory navicular bone: This is the most common extra bone in the foot. When present, it is found in the arch of the foot on the inside, making the foot appear flat. [See FIGURE 36.] Some are not painful, but when they are, the pain is persistent and surgical removal can require a very long recovery.

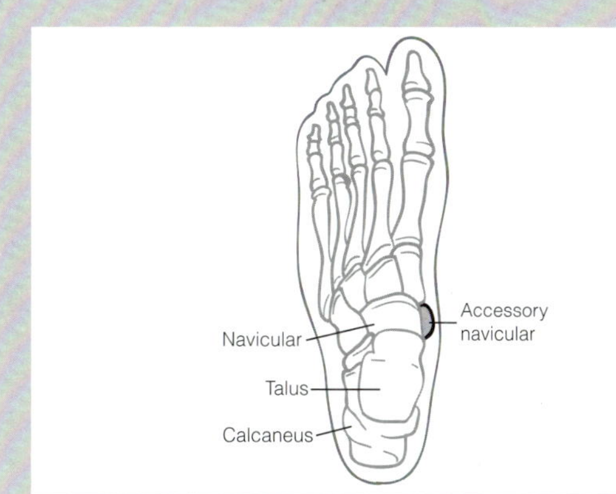

FIGURE 36. Accessory Navicular Bone (Left Foot, From Above)

Achilles tendonitis: The Achilles tendon can become inflamed and sore. [See FIGURE 35.] In younger individuals this is most commonly due to overuse, especially in individuals who engage in sports that require a lot of jumping. When tendonitis is not treated properly, the Achilles tendon can occasionally rupture or tear completely. The symptoms of Achilles tendonitis include pain in the heel when walking or running. The tendon is usually painful, and the overlying skin may be warm and swollen.

Classic ankle sprain: When the foot and ankle are inverted, both of the major ligaments on the outside (lateral) of the ankle can be damaged or torn. This is referred to as a classic ankle sprain. [See FIGURE 34.]

High ankle sprains: Injuries to the syndesmosis (the ligaments that join the tibia and fibula just above the ankle) are referred to as "high" ankle sprains. They heal very slowly, in part because of the poor blood supply to the area. [See FIGURE 9.]

Os trigonum: Another extra bone which may be present in the foot is the os trigonum, which occurs in the back of the talus. [See FIGURE 37.] It may cause no symptoms, but when it does, the pain is present in the back of the ankle and is associated with pointing (plantar flexion). The os trigonum is a relatively common accessory bone that occurs in 8-10 percent of the population and 50 percent of the time is present in both ankles.

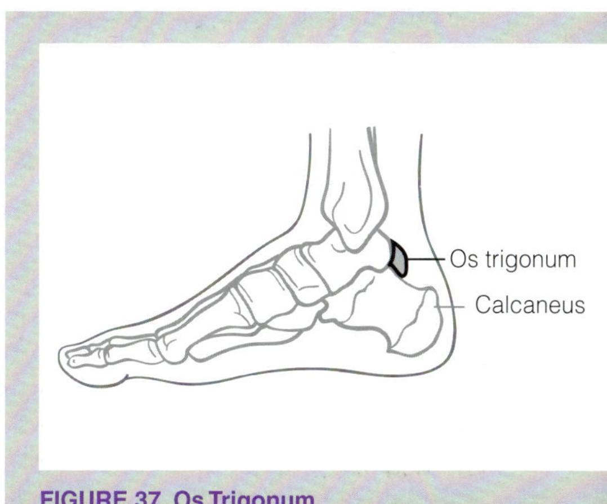

FIGURE 37. Os Trigonum (Right Foot, Medial View)

ELBOW

Dislocations of the elbow: Dislocations of the elbow can occur, but they are relatively uncommon. Dislocation would require a severe force—so much, in fact, that fractures often occur concurrently.

FOOT

Dancer's tendonitis: Occasionally, intense pointe work will cause the primary flexor tendon of the big toe (the FHL tendon) to develop tendonitis. [See FIGURE 29.] This injury is so specific to dancers that it is called "dancer's tendonitis." The FHL becomes inflamed as it passes behind the ankle and travels down into the foot toward the great toe. FHL tendonitis may manifest itself as inner (medial) or back (posterior) ankle pain, arch pain or big toe discomfort. The dancer may experience a "clicking" or locking sensation of the big toe.

Sesamoids: The sesamoids of the great toe can experience pain due to stress fractures or inflammation. [See FIGURE 4.] These two small bones inside of tendons (similar to miniature kneecaps) lie under the head of the first metatarsal bone just before the metatarsal-phalangeal joint itself. Most of the time they produce no symptoms. They can fracture either by a direct blow or by stress. They often heal slowly and, for reasons that are unknown, can die due to a loss of blood supply (avascular necrosis). If they fail to heal, they may need to be surgically removed.

Stress fractures: A stress fracture is a hairline crack in bone that develops as a result of repetitive stresses to the bone. The second metatarsal is most often associated with stress fractures in dancers because it is often the longest of the metatarsals and bears more force and weight than the others, especially on relevé.

HIP

Acetabular dysplasia: A shallow socket (acetabulum) can be associated with hip dislocation, labral tears and arthritis of the hip. [See FIGURE 38.] Some dancers are born with a shallow socket (acetabular dysplasia) and develop pain early in their training. Turnout can easily move the femoral head out of a shallow socket and lead to early wearing out of the hip joint ("degeneration"). These hips are prone to arthritis even without ballet training, so dancing may or may not exacerbate the condition.

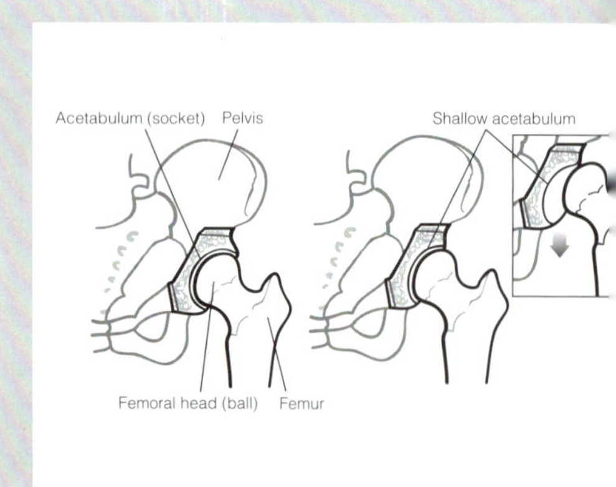

FIGURE 38. Acetabular Dysplasia (Left Hip, Front View)

Anteversion ("pigeon toes"): Excessive inward turning of the femur, called anteversion or "pigeon toes," may prevent adequate turnout in a dancer. People are born with one of three kinds of hips, which will determine the way they walk: normal (equal turn in and turnout); anteverted ("pigeon toed," which is increased turn in and decreased turnout); and retroverted ("duck footed," which is increased turnout and decreased turn in). It is very difficult to change these configurations, even by early training and capsular stretch. Normal hips will attain fair turnout. Retroverted hips will turn out well, and anteverted hips will turn out poorly. Other limitations in turnout may be related to strong and tight capsular ligaments.

Hip dislocations: Unlike the shoulder, the hip is rarely subject to dislocation, except in situations where the socket (acetabulum) is severely malformed and shallow (acetabular dysplasia), or following severe trauma, such as a motor vehicle accident.

Labral tears of the hip: The hip socket has a cartilaginous lip (labrum) that is thought to add increased depth to the socket. This labrum can be torn either by an acute injury or by forcing turnout. [See FIGURE 39.] A torn labrum causes pain and snapping in the groin that is often mistaken for iliopsoas tendonitis. [See FIGURE 22.] Labral tears sometimes require arthroscopic surgery if they don't respond to rest and physical therapy.

KNEE

Dislocations of the patella: Hypermobile individuals may be subject to dislocations of the patella, especially if there is an underlying problem with patellar alignment and they are turning out through or below the knee. If a dancer has poor turnout at the hip, but the foot is turned out below the knee to gain fifth position, the knee is caught between a turned-in hip and a turned-out foot. This is not good for the knee, which is designed more or less as a hinge joint and is not meant to rotate. [See FIGURE 8.] In addition, if the kneecap (patella) is loosely anchored (because of hypermobility) and the thigh muscles are weak, this can cause the patella to slip laterally (outward) out of its groove on the thigh bone (femur). If the patella slips out and then slips back in again, it is called a subluxation. If it goes all the way out and has to be put back by a doctor in an emergency room, it is called a dislocation. For a dislocation to occur, the ligaments that stabilize the kneecap and hold it in place must be torn. This makes the likelihood of recurrence very high and many surgeons recommend that the loose ligaments following dislocations be surgically repaired. Fortunately, most dance injuries are subluxations and not dislocations.

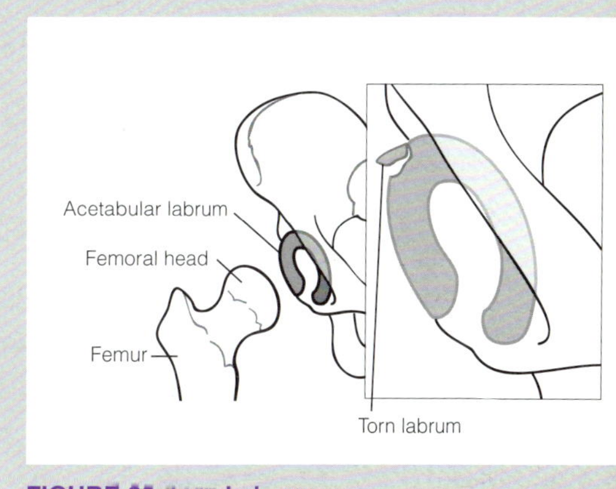

FIGURE 39. Torn Labrum (Right Hip, Front View)

Malalignment: Pain around the patella is occasionally a sign that the patella is not aligned properly and may be tracking off-center (typically toward the outside). Patellar malalignment is very common in female athletes because their hips are placed farther apart for child-bearing. The knees have to come together below, so there is a natural valgus (knock-knee) in females that contributes to this syndrome. Knee pain in females due to malalignment is so common in sports medicine that it has been referred to as "the miserable or malicious malalignment syndrome." [See FIGURE 40.]

Medial collateral ligament (MCL) and anterior cruciate ligament (ACL) tears: All four ligaments of the knee can be torn with severe knee injuries, but the most commonly injured are the medial collateral ligament (MCL) and anterior cruciate ligament (ACL). [See FIGURE 26.] ACL tears occur more commonly in women and may be seen in contact and non-contact injuries. Coming to a quick stop, combined with a change in direction while running, pivoting, landing from a jump or hyper-extending the knee, can result in ACL injuries. Oftentimes, the injury occurs with a popping sound, followed by severe pain and swelling. ACL injuries are often associated with injuries to the MCL. Following treatment, if instability persists after leg strength and knee motion have returned, major reconstructive surgery may be required.

Meniscal tears: Menisci are subject to tears with any stressful activity or force on the knee, particularly twisting or over-flexing the knee. [See FIGURE 41.] Symptoms of a meniscus tear depend on the size and location of the tear and whether other knee injuries occurred along with it. The pain is due to the swelling and injury to the surrounding tissues. Depending on the severity of the tear, patients may experience catching or locking of the knee. Meniscus tears may also produce a sensation of "giving way" or buckling. Depending upon the severity of the tear and the associated symptoms, arthroscopic surgery may be required.

Osgood Schlatter's disease: Osgood Schlatter's disease is one of the most common causes of knee pain in adolescents. [See FIGURE 42.] Consisting of pain and swelling of the tibial tubercle at the insertion of the patellar tendon, it is generally a benign condition that occurs when the tibial tubercle becomes repeatedly stressed from jumping.

Turning out from the knee: Too much rotation through the knee (as when forcing turnout) is especially harmful, since excessive rotation will strain the ligaments of the knee, and may subject both the menisci and articular cartilage to tear.

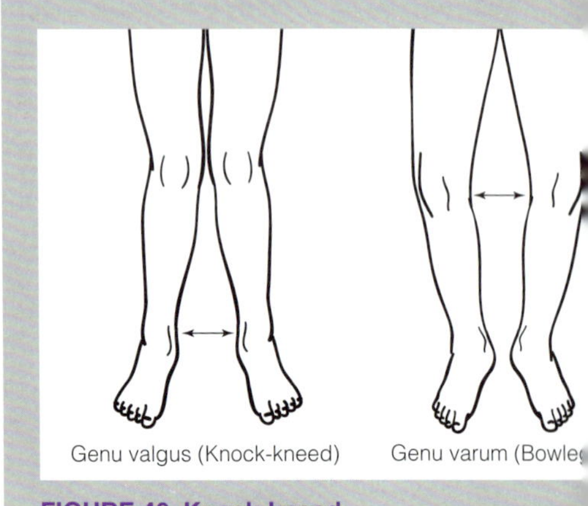

FIGURE 40. Knock-kneed and Bowlegged

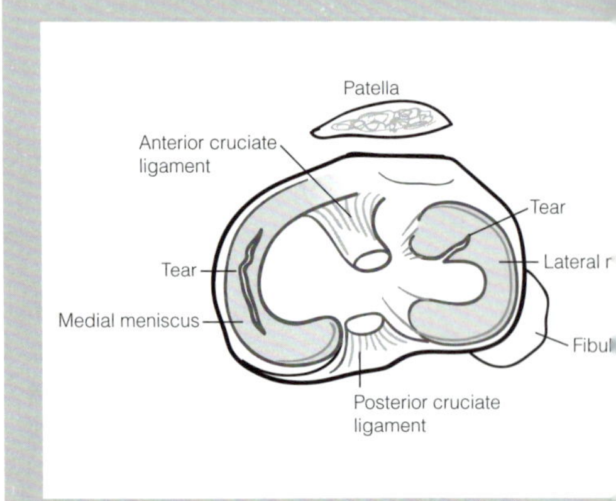

FIGURE 41. Torn Menisci (Right Knee, From Above)

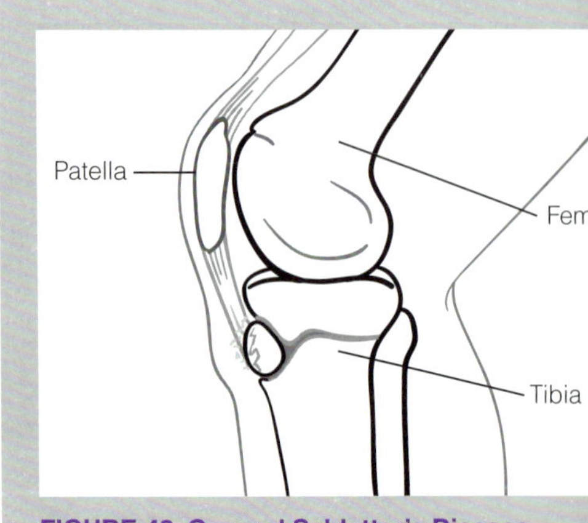

FIGURE 42. Osgood Schlatter's Disease (Right Knee, Medial View)

SHOULDER

Glenoid labrum tear: The glenoid labrum can be torn during a dislocation, or with other forces, and may lead to chronic instability or pain within the shoulder joint. [See FIGURE 43.]

Rotator cuff injuries: These are rare among dancers. The rotator cuff is an important tendon within the shoulder that stabilizes the head of the humerus in the socket of the glenoid on the scapula. [See FIGURE 31.] It enables the major muscles of the shoulder (such as the deltoid) to work efficiently. In older weekend athletes and baseball pitchers, the rotator cuff can wear out or develop small tears that cause pain and weakness. On rare occasions, male dancers can strain their rotator cuffs partnering and may have to avoid lifting until they heal. Male dancers and some females who are very loose-jointed are much more likely to have trouble with instability (subluxation) of the shoulder, where the humeral head tends to slip out of the glenoid in certain positions or lifts. On rare occasions this may need to be fixed by arthroscopic surgery.

Shoulder dislocation: The shoulder can dislocate—completely separating the ball from the socket—with severe force or trauma, or even with minor force if the individual is hypermobile.

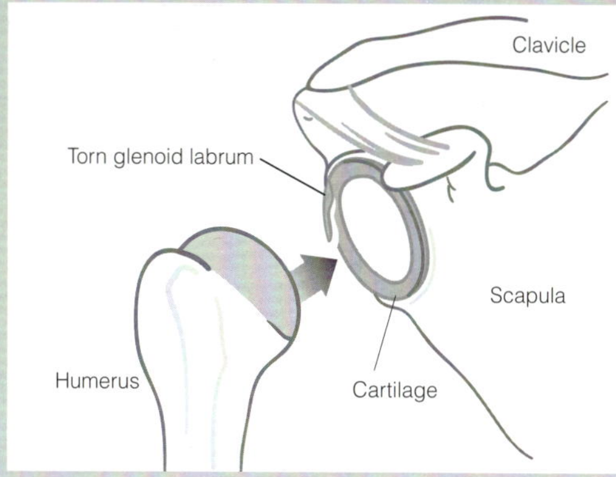

FIGURE 43. Torn Labrum (Right Shoulder, Front View)

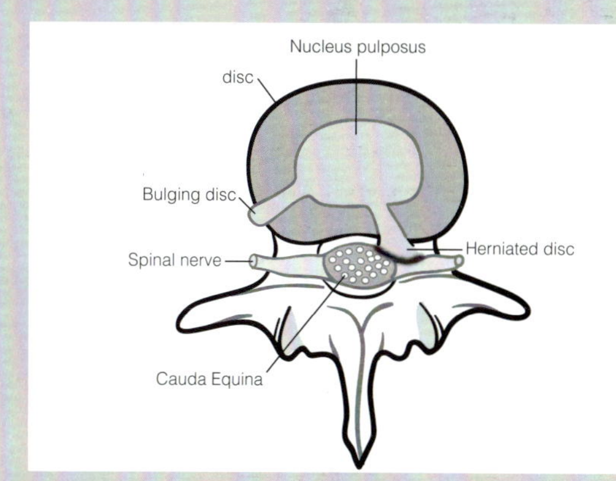

FIGURE 44. Herniated and Bulging Disc (From Above)

SPINE AND SPINAL CONSIDERATIONS

Truly serious spinal injuries—such as those that result in spinal cord damage—are rare in dance. However, because extreme ranges of motion are required in all segments of the dancer's spine, injury is always possible. If a dancer has a pre-existing or acquired spinal condition that results in a decreased range of motion, the adjacent spinal segments have to compensate by increasing their movement requirements. This compensation may result in increased musculoskeletal demands that can lead to further injury.

Disc herniation: The discs between the vertebrae can be subject to injury when the outside ring tears or ruptures and the softer central material squeezes out of the disc and presses against a nerve. [See FIGURE 44.] This can cause nerve pain down the leg, numbness and weakness. The term "sciatica" is often used to describe this condition. If a disc herniation is suspected, the dancer should see a physician as soon as possible. An MRI may be required.

Fused Vertebrae: Though it is rare, two vertebrae can develop as one fused vertebra (fusing to each other). This may limit spinal flexibility.

Kyphosis: When the thoracic spine is normally aligned, there is a slight forward bending. When the flexion is exaggerated, it is referred to as kyphosis. [See FIGURE 45.] Kyphosis can be caused by a variety of conditions including developmental problems, trauma, various diseases or degenerative disorders. In addition to decreased flexibility of the spine, individuals with kyphosis may complain of mild back pain.

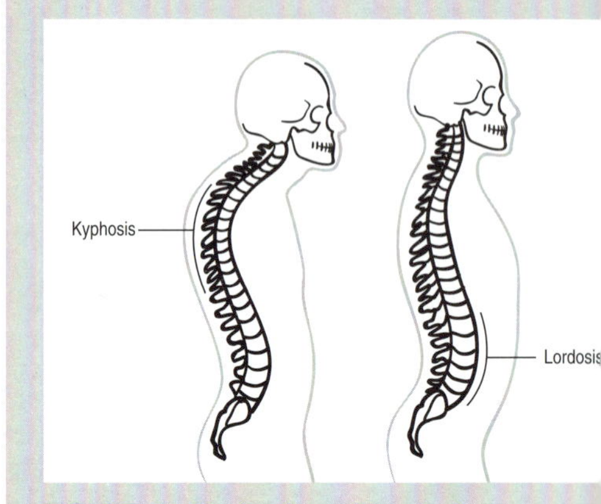

FIGURE 45. Kyphosis and Lordosis

Lordosis: Normal spine alignment also includes a backward bending or extension of the lumbar spine. When it is exaggerated, it is called lordosis. [See FIGURE 45.] Too much lordotic curving is referred to as swayback and may result in round shoulders and make the buttocks appear prominent. When lying on his/her back on a hard surface, a child with significant lordosis will have a space beneath his/her lower back and the surface.

Scoliosis: Scoliosis is a sideways curvature of the spine. [See FIGURE 46.] While scoliosis can be caused by a number of medical conditions, most of the time there is no known cause, and it is quite common in adolescent female ballet dancers. A thorough annual physical examination by the dancer's pediatrician or primary care physician should screen for the presence of these curves. Mild scoliosis is generally not a significant hindrance to ballet training; however, it means that the dance teacher should be especially vigilant about the dancer using proper technique. Teachers should be aware that the current "gold standard" for treatment of scoliotic curves that are greater than 20 degrees in growing children and adolescents is bracing and exercise. Unfortunately, neither therapeutic exercise alone nor manual/manipulative therapy will control these curves.

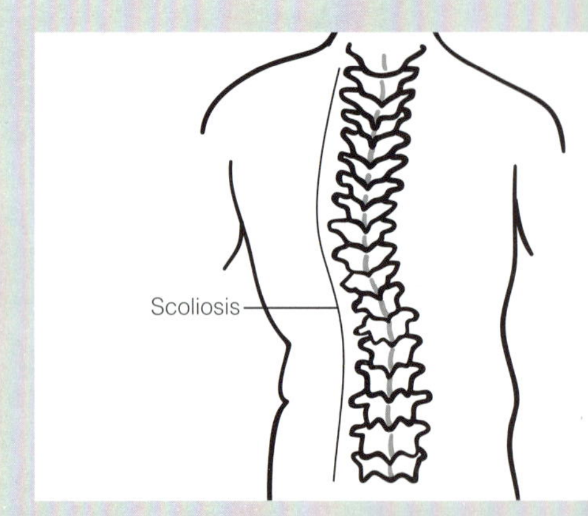

FIGURE 46. Scoliosis

Swayback and Stress Fractures

It is important to eliminate faulty technique (in both beginning and advanced students) that can result in lordosis. [See FIGURE 45.] Besides being aesthetically unpleasing, excessive lordosis may predispose the teenaged dancer (almost always female) to stress fracture(s) of the lower (lumbar) spine. Delayed onset of menstruation will increase the likelihood of developing this problem. Delayed menstruation is often caused by decreased estrogen, which is essential for the development and maintenance of healthy bones.

As male students mature, they are often required to perform a great deal of partnering. It is critical for the male dancer to control lordosis and use correct technique when lifting his partner. Male students should be encouraged to participate in core and upper-body strengthening programs.

Arabesque and Stress Fractures

The arabesque position requires simultaneous spinal hyperextension, rotation and side bending. It is important that all students learn the proper execution of this movement, which is to keep the hips level and extend the line from the hip. Students with insufficient hip extension will need to accept a less than optimal arabesque. Recurrent or persistent low back pain with the arabesque or attitude is a cardinal sign of a vertebral stress fracture.

Adolescent students may suddenly lose the height of their arabesque as they go through a growth spurt. The dance teacher should encourage these students to temporarily accept a lowered arabesque in order to avoid a subsequent permanent technical fault.

COMMON MEDICAL PROBLEMS—NOT DANCER-SPECIFIC

First aid principles are generally the same for all young dancers, male and female. However, musculoskeletal injuries are best treated according to age or age group, since injuries vary according to the stage of growth and development.

Abrasion: Raw, superficial skin wounds resulting from sliding on a rough floor or Marley should be cleansed thoroughly with soap and water. Gently scrub the area to remove all visible dirt—this will help prevent permanent tattooing of the skin as well as lower the risk of infection. Then apply a sterile bandage or band-aid. (Advise the students to be certain that they are up-to-date with their tetanus toxoid immunization by checking with their physician. This immunization should be good for 10 years.)

Allergic reactions: Allergic reactions can be unexpected and very frightening. A dancer who is allergic to nuts can react to something as simple as eating a granola bar that was made in a factory that also processes nuts. Even eating a sauce or salad dressing that has been made with pine nuts, almonds or peanuts can cause a serious allergic reaction. An early sign of an allergic reaction may be a rash or hives, or the dancer's face may begin to turn pink and swell. The airway can begin to narrow, leading to wheezing and shortness of breath followed by a drop in blood pressure and fainting. Any dancer with a significant allergy to a food or to stinging insects should carry an EpiPen. If there are young children with these allergies in the dance school, it's a good idea to learn how to use the EpiPen in case of an emergency. The dance student and/or parent should inform the teacher of any significant allergies. Don't hesitate to call 911 if an allergic reaction appears to be serious.

Asthma: Asthma is a very common problem among children. Dancers needing inhalers should always carry them in their dance bag. Inhalers are typically used before dance class begins.

Blister: Blisters may be prevented if attended to as soon as discomfort is noticed. They occur when something (a pointe shoe, for example) repetitively rubs against the skin, causing the layers of skin to separate. One or more layers of fabric between the rubbing object and the skin allows sliding of the fabric layers rather than blistering of the skin. A thin silicone or gel pad can reduce the friction that causes blisters and provide padding for additional comfort. Once a blister forms, it's best to leave it intact until it breaks spontaneously. However, in some situations it's better to drain a large blister under sterile conditions and then protect it (as above). If in doubt about whether to leave it or drain it, check with a healthcare professional. If there is any opening of the skin, wash the area with soap and water and consider applying a topical antibiotic like Neosporin.

Broken tooth: If a dancer breaks a tooth at or near the root, find it and send him/her to seek emergency care. Place the tooth in a small, clean cup of either pasteurized milk or special transport fluid, which is sold specifically as tooth transport fluid in some first-aid kits. If neither milk nor transport fluid is available, the student can hold the tooth in his/her mouth. Re-implantation of a tooth has the best chance of success within the first few hours.

Bumps and bruises: Most skin bumps and bruises respond best when treated immediately with ice or other cold therapy. They usually resolve within a few days without further treatment.

Concussion: When a dancer's head hits the floor, another object or a fellow dancer, a brain injury called a concussion may occur. A concussion can happen without the dancer ever losing consciousness. However, even mild brain injury may alter the dancer's balance, agility and quickness. It may also decrease his/her attentiveness and ability to focus, make the dancer "cranky" and/or interfere with sleep patterns.

More serious head injuries can cause a loss of consciousness. Seizures may also occur at this time, depending on the extent of the injury. The dancer who is unconscious from a head injury should not be moved because the trauma that injured the head may also have injured the neck. In this situation, only a trained professional should move the dancer. Call 911 immediately.

A dancer with any significant head injury, even one that does not cause loss of consciousness, must have an appropriate medical evaluation by a physician before returning to dance, in order to avoid further damage. The student should provide a written note from his/her physician stating that it is appropriate for him/her to return to dance.

Eye injury: Collision with a piece of scenery, another dancer's elbow or anything else can cause eye injury. If the area around the eye turns black and blue, it should be iced and evaluated medically to rule out a fracture. If blood is visible in the globe (eyeball), or if there is a change in the dancer's vision (blurry, flashing lights, etc.), emergency evaluation is required.

Feeling faint/fainting: Dancers may feel lightheaded or faint simply because they have not eaten sufficiently. (This can cause a drop in blood sugar called hypoglycemia.) A lack of glucose in the brain combined with the stress of a class or performance may cause a dancer to "gray out" or completely black out and lose consciousness. If a dancer begins to feel faint, s/he should lie down on the floor with the legs elevated above the level of the heart. Once the dancer is alert enough to sit in an upright position and drink, give him/her fluids. Orange juice is a good source of sugar that can be rapidly absorbed into the bloodstream.

A young dancer may also faint or lose consciousness because of a heart abnormality, though this is not very common. The student or parent should inform the teacher of any underlying heart problems (rhythm disturbances, valve abnormalities, etc.) that could potentially put the dancer at risk. If an automatic electronic defibrillator device is available at the studio, teachers should be trained to use it in case of an emergency. Emergency medical help is required and should be obtained by calling 911.

Infectious disease (skin, pink eye): Dancers are constantly touching barres, floors and each other during class and rehearsal, and that's all it takes to spread infectious skin diseases such as impetigo, foot fungal infections or herpes. One particular skin infection of special concern, because of its resistance to commonly used antibiotics, is called MRSA (methicillin resistant staphylococcus aureus). To prevent these infections, dancers should wash their hands frequently with soap and water. They should not share soap with others and should get examined if they have sores that are swollen, red, painful or draining pus. Cuts and scrapes should be kept clean and covered with bandages, and personal items such as towels and razors should not be shared. A sore or lesion needs to be touched directly for the herpes virus to be transmitted, but a dancer with pink eye who rubs his/her infected eye and then touches someone or something can pass it along. If in doubt, dancers with these disorders should check with their physician as to whether they are contagious and whether it is safe for them to be in a dance school environment. Personal cleanliness will help prevent the spread of some of these infections.

Laceration: Any cut that is deep, long or near a joint should be looked at immediately by a doctor. A small cut that is near a joint may appear innocuous, but if the laceration actually enters the joint it could potentially lead to a joint infection. A dancer with a grossly contaminated cut or puncture wound will need a tetanus injection if immunizations are not up-to-date.

Note: All blood should be cleaned up from the floor and barre according to the guidelines in Part 3: Risk-Management, Medical and Facility Guidelines.

Nose injury: Collision with a piece of scenery, another dancer's elbow or anything else can cause a nosebleed. A simple nosebleed can usually be controlled by pinching the nose firmly between the thumb and forefinger while applying ice. The student should be kept sitting up. Persistent bleeding necessitates medical attention. A broken nose should be evaluated within 24 hours to optimize cosmetic and functional results.

Splinter: A splinter may be removed with tweezers or lifted out of the skin with a sterile needle. Deep, large splinters may require medical attention and should not be left in the skin to fester. The splinter wound should be thoroughly cleaned. Consider applying a topical antibiotic such as Neosporin.

CHAPTER 3: Injury Prevention and Recovery

PREVENTION OF DANCE INJURY

Total prevention of all injuries is unrealistic. The dance teacher's goal should be to minimize injury rates as much as possible. This can be done if these guidelines are followed:

1. Make sure students have time to warm up.

Proper warm-up is essential in preventing injury. Recent studies in sports medicine have shown that warm-up should begin with slow/moderate activity, such as running, which uses major muscle groups, followed by appropriate stretching. The ideal time to stretch is between barre and center exercises. That practice should be encouraged and ample time should be provided. Dancers often stretch before class and although there are no deleterious effects to this time-honored practice, overly aggressive stretching and/or bouncing while stretching should be avoided to prevent injury.

2. Be realistic.

Young students should be discouraged from attempting positions and movements they aren't ready for. Teachers must not place students in positions that may be extreme and potentially injurious. Class should be designed to avoid overworking a specific part of the body (such as the calf or hip). An overly competitive class environment can also lead to injury and should be discouraged. Attention to proper alignment (avoiding excessive lordosis/swayback, aligning knees over second toes in plié, etc.) from the beginning can prevent injuries in the long run.

3. Keep a safe studio.

Environmental factors are key to preventing injuries. A safe studio includes sprung, level dance floors; Marleys that are not overly slippery or sticky; and good lighting. Additionally, classes should not be overly crowded.

4. Avoid overworking the boys.

Male students are often in short supply and teachers must avoid requiring excessive partnering. Boys should be encouraged to participate in upper-body and core strengthening programs outside of dance school before initiating serious partnering.

5. Be smart about summer intensives.

Summer intensive programs create physical challenges for students, teachers and organizers. These particular programs schedule up to four dance classes per day for a student population who may be averaging only four classes or less per week. It is important that the increase in load be ramped to avoid high rates of student injury and frustration. Ideally, students should start intensives by taking no more than two classes a day, increasing by one class every two days if no injuries or extreme muscle soreness occur. To fill the void from fewer dance classes during the first few days of an intensive, add core strengthening sessions, floor barre, Pilates, mat classes and lectures on proper nutrition.

RETURNING TO DANCE FOLLOWING INJURY: GUIDING A STUDENT BACK TO CLASS

A dance student returning to ballet class after an injury faces many challenges—most importantly, how his/her body will readjust to being in the studio again. It is the dance teacher's responsibility to guide him/her through the process. This can be done by following four guidelines:

1. Communicate with doctors.

Before an injured student returns to class, his/her dance teacher should communicate with the dancer's physicians and/or physical therapists to determine if the student is ready to resume dancing and if there are elements or portions of class that s/he should avoid.

2. Take it slowly.

Typically, a returning student should perform only a partial barre for the first week, and then when s/he is ready, s/he can progress to a full barre and then center. The returning student must be encouraged to focus on placement and technique. Slow and steady progression in a non-competitive atmosphere is essential for a successful recovery.

3. Get feedback.

The dance teacher should seek feedback from the student to gauge appropriate progression and consult with the student's clinicians if necessary. The student should be encouraged to take responsibility for his/her recovery, which means that the student's concerns must be respected and responded to appropriately. (For example, the dancer should verbalize whether the progression of dance activity is too fast or too slow.) A dancer who has sustained a foot or ankle injury should not resume pointe work until full range of motion and strength has returned.

4. Get to know local dance doctors and other health professionals with expertise in dance medicine.

It is helpful for the dance teacher to establish relationships with physicians and physical therapists in the local area with experience in dance medicine. If there are none, it is useful to invite clinicians to observe class whenever possible. In this way, the clinician can slowly learn the elements and demands of class and better prepare and guide an injured student's return to dance class.

CHAPTER 4: Turnout

INTRODUCTION

Proper turnout is not only the cornerstone of correct ballet technique, it is also essential in minimizing the risk of injury. [See PHOTO 2.]

A dancer's turnout comes from two areas: above the knee and below the knee. The turnout at the hip joint provides most of the external rotation above the knee, but the knee and shin (tibia) turn out slightly below the knee as well. The motion is rarely the same on both sides. Different combinations can provide the classic fifth position. As all dance teachers know, the turnout in ballet should come from the hip and not the knee. Forcing turnout below the knee is the most common technical mistake seen in ballet and is the cause of many, if not most, injuries. One hundred and eighty degrees of turnout from the hips is extremely rare and students will commonly compensate by adopting one or more of the following strategies.

IMPROPER TURNOUT

Common misalignments to increase turnout include:

- **Lordosis:** Dancers (especially young ones) try to increase their turnout by adopting a posture of increased lordosis, or swayback (sticking out their buttocks). This posture places abnormal stresses on the lower back and can lead to stress fractures and other problems of the lower spine. [See PHOTO 3.]
- **"Screwing out" at the knee:** When a dancer's toes are perfectly turned to the side and his/her knees are facing front, s/he is "screwing out" at the knee. This is probably the most common incorrect method of increasing turnout. The knee joint is a modified hinge joint and is not designed to rotate. Over time, these rotational forces can lead to kneecap (patellar) problems, cartilage (meniscus) tears and eventual degenerative arthritis of the knee. [See PHOTO 4.]
- **Pronation:** "Rolling in" excessively at the foot and ankle is another common fault utilized to increase total turnout. Excessive "rolling in" (or pronation) can lead to a variety of injuries throughout the lower extremities. [See PHOTO 5.]

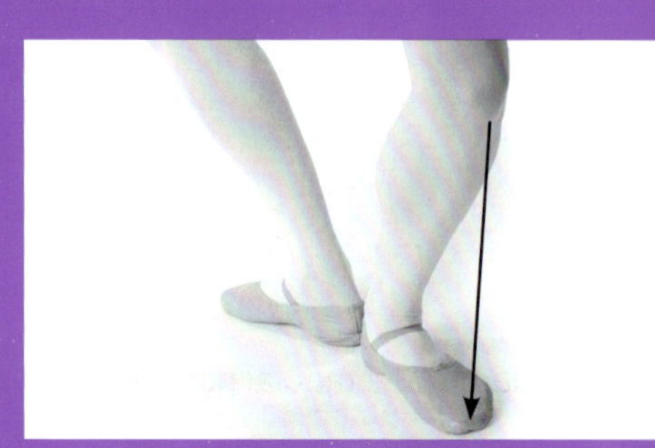

PHOTO 2. Proper Turnout

CORRECT | INCORRECT

PHOTO 3. Lordosis

CORRECT | INCORRECT

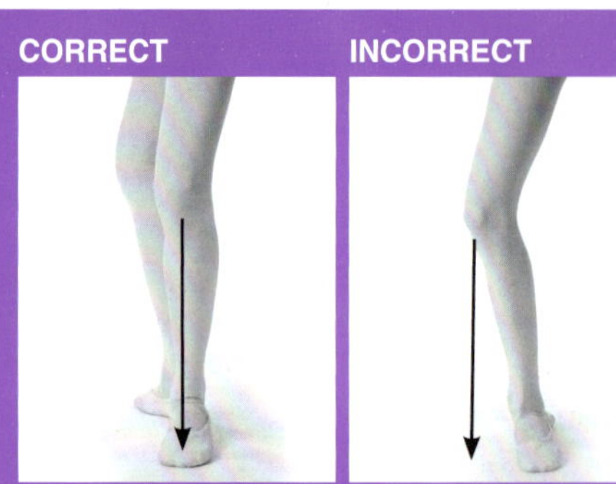

PHOTO 4. "Screwing out" at the knee

INCORRECT

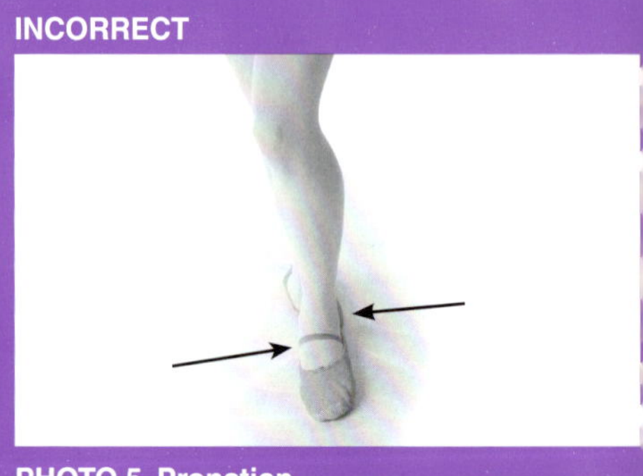

PHOTO 5. Pronation

TURNOUT ASSESSMENT

There is a simple way to assess if a student is working his/her turnout correctly and safely: Ask the student to stand in a first position demi-plié. The tip of the kneecap should be directly over the first and second metatarsals in the foot. While this will very rarely allow 180 degrees of turnout, it will most certainly yield healthier dancers.

In pre-professional students, however, the increased expectations for something closer to 180-degree turnout may mean allowing the knees to be over any part of the medial part of the foot, within a safe range. [See PHOTO 6.]

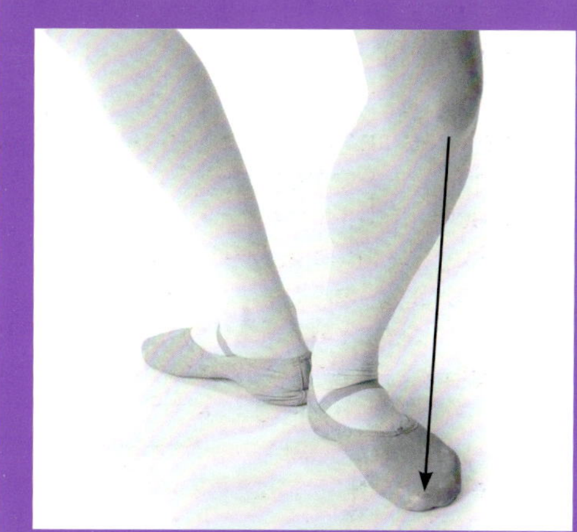

PHOTO 6. Turnout Assessment

INCREASING TURNOUT

Students frequently want to know if and how they can increase their hip turnout. While it is possible, any change in the hip's natural ability to rotate will only be minimal.

Babies are generally born pigeon-toed (anteverted), which usually decreases slowly until the age of 10-12. So there may be a "natural" increase in hip turnout during that time. However, orthopedic literature suggests that the final degree of turnout and turn in is genetically predetermined and cannot be altered easily, if at all. Overly aggressive attempts to increase hip turnout can result in permanent and/or future damage to the hip joints. That said, if a dancer is taught to work properly with the natural turnout s/he possesses, s/he can gain the desired aesthetic and more of the freedom of movement that turnout allows the legs.

SAFE TURNOUT EXERCISES

Younger dancers (up to age 12) can increase hip turnout safely by doing the lunge stretch and frog stretch. When done properly, these exercises may stretch the soft tissue structures (the ligaments) in the front of the hip joint enough to allow a few additional degrees of hip turnout. But be careful: These stretches can result in injury if done in an extreme or overly aggressive manner. [See PHOTOS 7, 8 and 9.]

LUNGE STRETCH

When done properly, the lunge stretch may increase hip turnout by a couple of degrees. This is accomplished by prudently stretching the anterior capsule of the hip joint, as shown. [See PHOTOS 7 and 8.]

This stretch can be done up to twice daily with the stretch being held for up to two minutes. The lunge stretch should never produce pain during or after the stretch.

Performing this stretch in the presence of pain, with bouncing or with an external force through the hip joint could potentially lead to serious injury.

PHOTO 7. Starting Position for Lunge Stretch

FROG STRETCH

The frog stretch is used by some dancers in an attempt to improve turnout. Although it could increase a dancer's turnout slightly, we urge caution in doing this stretch because it may put excessive stress on the anterior capsule of the hip, which can lead to permanent injury. This is especially true if the dancer forces his/her range of motion to achieve the position. If the position is uncomfortable or does not feel like a muscular stretch, then the dancer can straighten his/her knees slightly or lie in a similar position on his/her back. [See PHOTO 9.]

PHOTO 8. Final Position for Lunge Stretch

PHOTO 9. Frog Stretch

CHAPTER 5: Introducing Pointe Work

INITIATING POINTE WORK

Before tackling the question of the proper age to begin pointe work, a brief discussion of the physical prerequisites required for pointe work is warranted.

PHYSICAL PREREQUISITES

At a minimum, the foot en pointe should be in a vertical position. [See PHOTO 11.] Anything less than vertical requires musculoskeletal demands that most certainly will lead to injury and will markedly limit the ability to function on pointe.

For the foot to achieve the vertical position on pointe there must be enough mobility in the foot and ankle to allow the foot to move all the way over onto the pointe. The greater the student's hyperextension of the knee, the greater the range of motion required in the foot and ankle to compensate and achieve this position of the foot. If the foot and ankle are too stiff or restricted, the student will have trouble getting up onto the tip of the pointe shoe. [See PHOTO 12.]

Since the ability to achieve a full relevé on pointe requires at least 90 degrees of foot and ankle motion (from the flex to the point), an effective way for the teacher to evaluate a student's range of motion is to look at the feet when the student is on relevé in second position. In this position, the feet should extend into a straight line with the shin. [See PHOTO 10.]

PHOTO 10. 2nd Position Relevé with Dancer's Right Foot at 90 Degrees and Left Foot at Less than 90

PHOTO 11. 90 Degrees of Foot and Ankle Motion On Pointe

PHOTO 12. Less Than 90 Degrees of Foot and Ankle Motion On Pointe

THE AGE TO BEGIN

The traditional age for girls to begin pointe work has been in the 11- to 13-year-old range, since it was felt that younger dancers could injure the bony architecture of their feet by attempting pointe work prematurely. However, there is little evidence to support this concept. It is known that three to four years of early ballet training are necessary for a dancer to achieve the required strength, balance and coordination needed for purposeful pointe work. Prolonged early training also serves to slowly introduce stresses to the bones of the feet, allowing them to build strength and density. Medically, this is known as Wolf's Law, which states that a healthy bone will adapt to the load that is placed on it. If loading on a particular bone increases, the bone will remodel itself over time to become stronger and more able to resist that sort of loading.

TEACHER KNOWS BEST

A student who began relatively serious training at the age of 8 or 9—and who has the necessary prerequisite range of motion in her feet and ankles—is usually ready to begin pointe training at the "traditional" age range of 11-13. However, problems arise for the adolescent female who begins dance training at an older age. Since the majority of her peers may have begun pointe work already, the late starter may put tremendous pressure on her teacher to allow her to do likewise. Teachers must remember that the strength, balance, coordination and skeletal development required for safe pointe work will take years, not months, for the late starter to develop. This time frame can sometimes be shortened for adolescents who have an extensive background in rhythmic or traditional gymnastics, as many of the neuro-developmental and musculoskeletal demands are similar. Children mature and develop at different rates, so some will be ready before others.

Ultimately, an experienced dance teacher who sees students several times each week is in the best position to know when it is appropriate for a young dancer to begin pointe work.

POINTE SHOE FITTING

This event is certainly one of the high points in a young dancer's career, and it should be fun and enjoyable. The dance teacher should play a major role in the selection of the toe shoe. There are many different manufacturers and types of shoes available, with variations in toe shape, vamp and insole, so each student will need help knowing what is best for her.

PREPARING THE SHOES

A young dancer must be shown how to sew on the ribbons and elastics, and how to properly tie the ribbons around her ankles. [See PHOTO 13.] To protect the toes, lamb's wool, paper towels and/or toe pads can be worn. Special padding may be needed if the dancer has unequal toe length or deformities such as bunions. Be aware that too much padding or too solid a toe box can take away the "feel of the floor," or proprioception, that a dancer needs. Once the shoes are sewn and ready to be used, they must be worn gradually to break them in, and to allow calluses to form on the toes to avoid blisters. Just walking around in them at home can toughen up and strengthen the feet. All of this preparation rapidly becomes a labor of love.

THREE TIPS FOR TRYING ON NEW POINTE SHOES

- Buy new shoes late in the day, when the feet are larger.
- A dancer should always try on new shoes in the tights and with the padding she will be wearing in the shoe.
- Toe shoes should be resized at least every three years throughout a dancer's career, even after growth is over. Even in adulthood the feet continue to spread. Resizing should be done even more frequently during adolescent growth spurts.

New shoes should be purchased when...

- ...the dancer's old pair no longer fits properly.
- ...the shoes have softened so much that they no longer provide proper support to the foot on pointe. Usually the tip of the pointe shoe or the shank of the shoe weakens, or "dies," first.

PHOTO 13. Example of How to Correctly Tie Pointe Shoe Ribbon

CHAPTER 6: Screening For Pre-Professionals

As dance training progresses in adolescence, a time comes when dancers have to decide how serious they are about a potential career as a professional. This is a big and complicated decision and should be made in consultation with the student's parents and dance teacher.

The two most important factors in this decision are (1) a dancer's talent, and (2) if ballet is the goal, whether s/he has the appropriate body. For a professional ballet dancer, having the appropriate body can mean the difference between a career marred by multiple injuries or one relatively free of these burdens. A trip to a dance medicine orthopedist or physical therapist can help in the decision-making process. There is a relatively simple screening used at ABT to look for problems or deficiencies that can be worked on through physical therapy to reduce or prevent injuries. To download a form to take to your orthopedist that describes the screening exam, please visit the ABT website, www.abt.org, or contact ABT at 212-477-3030.

Unfortunately, not everyone can be a professional ballet dancer. Beginning a pre-professional training program with a body not suited for ballet will likely lead to a career of injuries and disappointments. This does not mean that a talented dancer can't have a successful dance career in other forms of dance and performance, and he/she should be encouraged to pursue one.

CHAPTER 7: A Glossary Of Dance Medicine Terms

A.

Accessory navicular bone: The accessory navicular bone is the most common extra bone in the foot. When present, it is found in the medial (inside) arch of the foot, making the foot appear flat. Some are not painful, but when they are, the pain is persistent and surgical removal can require a very long recovery. [See FIGURE 36.]

Achilles tendon: The Achilles tendon is the largest tendon in the body and connects the calf muscles to the heel bone (the calcaneus). [See FIGURE 1.] It can be strained and develop tendonitis, either in the tendon itself or in its insertion into the heel. [See FIGURE 35.] In older male dancers it can tear or rupture. This is a devastating injury and often occurs in the twilight of a professional career. In a serious dancer or athlete it requires surgery. Unfortunately, this surgery has a high complication rate and a long recovery.

Anterior: The front of the body or body part.

Anterior cruciate ligament (ACL): The ACL is a ligament within the knee that provides stability for movements that require turning. [See FIGURE 26.] Rupture of this ligament has become an all-too-common injury in sports, and women are especially vulnerable. While ACL injuries are not common in dancers, when they occur, they usually leave the knee unstable and require surgery.

Anteversion: This term is used to describe natural inward rotation of the femur. Children who have a lot of anteversion are referred to as being "pigeon-toed." Their feet turn inward and it is very difficult for them to achieve sufficient turnout for ballet. It is very important that they work with their natural physicality. The most common fault in ballet technique is forcing an anteverted hip to achieve full turnout. The opposite of anteversion is retroversion.

Apophysis: A projection or outgrowth on a growing bone that is usually the site of the insertion or origin of a muscle or tendon (e.g., tibial tubercle). [See FIGURE 25.]

Arch types: Feet have one of three arch types: a normal arch, a flat foot and a high arched, or cavus, foot. [See FIGURE 47.] Dancers usually have a high arch. While a high arch is desirable for a good relevé, this foot is rigid and absorbs energy poorly, so it is prone to sprains and stress fractures.

Atrophy: The wasting or lack of normal tone, size or strength, usually of a muscle. It is frequently a result of inactivity of the muscle or muscle group, and can be the result of a neurological disorder.

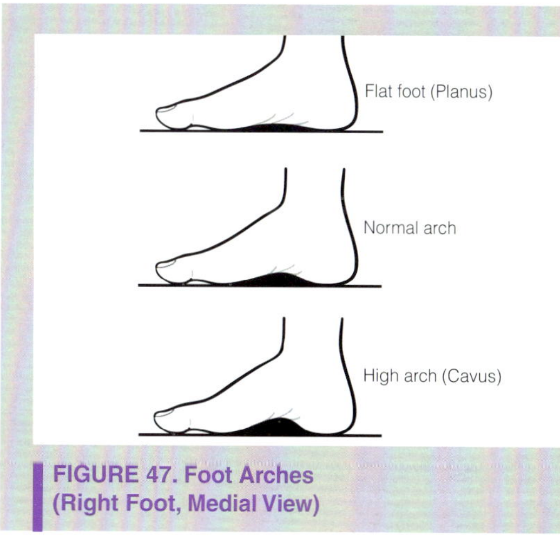

FIGURE 47. Foot Arches (Right Foot, Medial View)

B.

Bone scan: A radiology test performed to detect increased blood flow in a bone or joint. It will be called positive (or "hot") when a fracture, early arthritis or a bone tumor is present. It is very accurate in detecting these issues when regular X-rays cannot.

Bow legs, or genu varum: Bow legs are desirable in ballet dancers because they are more aesthetic and make a better fifth position. George Balanchine much preferred these over the opposite, knock-knees, or genu valgum. [See FIGURE 40.]

Bunions: An inherited disorder that causes a deformity of the big toe joint (1ST metatarsal-phalangeal joint, or 1ST MPJ). Bunions sometimes begin in adolescence. A bony mass forms on the medial side of the joint, and the big toe (hallux) drifts toward the little toe (valgus). This deformity is not caused by dancing or the ballet toe shoe. It has been shown that bunions are no more common in ballet dancers than in the general population. Serious dancers should avoid bunion surgery until they retire because this surgery usually causes stiffness in the joint that can limit the demi-pointe relevé. Bunions are best managed by wide shoes and spacers between the first and second toes to maintain the alignment of the big toe.

C.

Calf strain, or "tennis leg": The calf has three muscles that join at the Achilles tendon. [See FIGURE 1.] The largest is the one on the inside of the calf, the "medial gastroc" (gastrocnemius). If this muscle is severely strained or "pulled," it can feel like being struck in the back of the leg. When this happens, it may indicate a complete rupture of the Achilles tendon itself. Fortunately, most calf strains aren't serious, though they can take a long time to heal.

Chiropractor: A manipulation/adjustment health-care provider who attended Chiropractic School (not medical school). They present themselves as Dr. (Name), leaving the patient to ascertain whether they are Medical Doctors (MDs), Doctors of Osteopathy (DOs) or Doctors of Chiropractics (DCs).

Chondromalacia: A softening of the under-surface (cartilage) of the kneecap where it rests against the underlying bone. This results in a noise called crepitus.

Compartment Syndromes: See "Leg pain."

Condyles: The rounded prominences at the end of a bone, such as the femur, that articulate with another bone. [See FIGURE 8.]

Crepitus: A grinding or crunching noise or sensation arising from under the kneecap as it moves up and down. It is the principal sign of chondromalacia. Some crepitus is normal, especially in older dancers. Painless crepitus is of no concern, but painful crepitus should be evaluated.

CT Scan (cat scan): A radiologic X-ray examination performed to evaluate problems that are primarily in the bones and less in the soft tissues (see "MRI").

D.

"Dancer's fracture of the foot": A fracture of the shaft of the fifth metatarsal (see "Fifth metatarsal").

"Dancer's tendonitis": A tendon called the flexor hallucis longus (FHL) that runs through a small tunnel on the inside of the back of the ankle frequently becomes strained and painful in female ballet dancers. It can become chronically inflamed and in some cases a dancer may need to have the tunnel surgically enlarged. [See FIGURE 29.]

"Degeneration": A medical euphemism for "wear and tear."

E.

Epiphysis: The growth plate at each end of a long bone. [See FIGURE 3.] It is present when the bone is growing in length and it disappears when the bone's growth phase is completed. The epiphysis is not as strong as the bone itself and is vulnerable to injury and overload, especially during periods of rapid growth, such as during adolescence, when it becomes wider and weaker.

Eversion: The outward movement of the heel and foot beneath the ankle. This occurs when rolling in or pronating the foot. [See FIGURE 13.]

F.

FHL: The flexor hallucis longus tendon running down the inside of the ankle. (See "Dancer's tendonitis.") [See FIGURE 29.]

Fibula: The bone running down the outside of the tibia in the lower leg. The lower one-third of this bone is another area where stress fractures occur, especially in dancers who pronate when they land or force their turnout. These fractures are easily seen on a bone scan. [See FIGURE 14.]

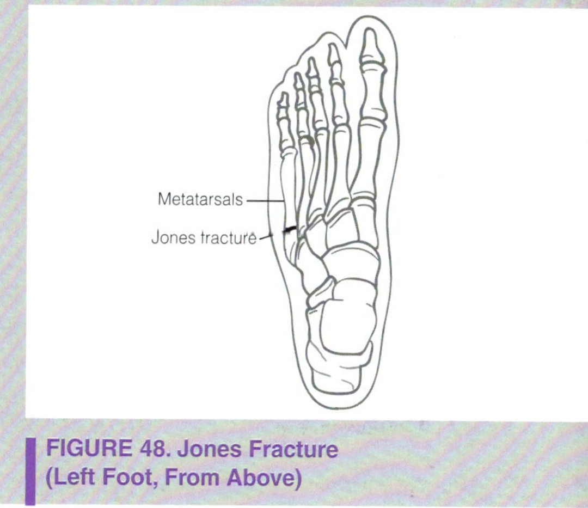

FIGURE 48. Jones Fracture (Left Foot, From Above)

Fifth (5TH) metatarsal: The outermost bone in the fore foot. It is frequently injured when the foot rolls inward when on relevé. All the weight goes onto the outside of the foot, and the bone is overloaded. It can fracture in four places, three of which are not serious and usually heal with immobilization, rarely requiring surgery. The serious injury is the "Jones fracture" that is in the proximal (nearer to the center of the body) one-third of the bone of the fifth metatarsal. It tends not to heal and frequently requires surgery, so it is important to know exactly what type of fracture has occurred. [See FIGURE 48.]

Foot: The foot is divided into three parts: the hind foot, mid foot and fore foot. [See FIGURE 19.] The long bones in the fore foot are called the metatarsals. They are numbered one through five beginning with the large one leading to the big toe. The base of the second metatarsal is a common location for stress fractures in female dancers, especially those with menstrual irregularities. This is different from a "dancer's fracture" involving the fifth metatarsal, noted above, which is an actual fracture and not a stress fracture.

Foot types: [See FIGURE 49.] The "Grecian" (or Morton's) foot is one where the second toe is the longest. The "Egyptian" foot is one where the great toe is the longest. The "Giselle" or "Peasant" foot is broad and square and is ideal for a dancer. The "Model" foot is narrow, tapered and poor for dancing because it does not provide a strong base on pointe or demi-pointe.

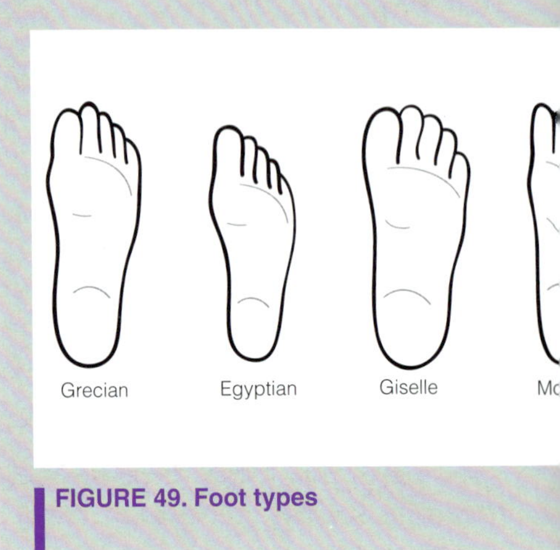

FIGURE 49. Foot types

G.

Genu valgum: Knock-kneed. [See FIGURE 40.]

Genu varum: Bowlegged. (See "Bow legs, or genu varum.") [See FIGURE 40.]

H.

Hallux rigidus: A painful stiffness that occurs in the big toe in the first metatarsal-phalangeal (1st MTP) joint when it wears out and slowly becomes arthritic. This is a difficult problem for a dancer because the demi-pointe relevé becomes painful. [See FIGURE 19.]

Hamstrings: [See FIGURE 24.] The hamstrings consist of three major muscles: the semitendinosus and the semimembranosus, which together make up the medial hamstring, and the biceps femoris, which is the lateral hamstring. The hamstrings control flexion of the knee and assist in extension of the hip (as in arabesque). Tightness in the hamstrings may prevent full flexion of the hip and full extension of the knee.

Hip: The hip is a ball and socket joint. The socket is centered in the pelvis and is called the acetabulum. [See FIGURE 6.] The ball is located on the top of the femur, or thigh bone. Some dancers are born with a shallow socket (acetabular dysplasia) and develop pain early in their training. This condition is one of the few contraindications for ballet because turnout can easily move the head out of a shallow socket and lead to early wearing out of the hip joint ("degeneration"). [See FIGURE 38.] Unfortunately, these hips are prone to arthritis even without ballet training.

Hyperextension: Backward curvature of a joint, such as the knee.

I.

Iliopsoas: A muscle that originates deep in the abdomen just in front of the lower spine and runs down the inner pelvis to insert in the upper thighbone (femur) just below the hip. [See FIGURE 22.] Although the iliopsoas muscle has a number of functions, its main function is to act as a hip flexor. A strain of the tendinous insertion of this muscle is usually the cause of the "groin pull." Iliopsoas tendonitis can be associated with a snapping sound caused as the iliotibial band snaps over the bony prominence (greater trochanter) of the femur. The snapping sound can be confused with the sound caused by a labral tear of the hip. [See FIGURE 39.]

Iliotibial band (ITB): The ITB is a thick band of connective tissue. It runs along the outside of the thigh from the crest of the ilium, over the lateral condyle of the femur, and inserts into the tibial tubercle.

Impingement: This happens when a tendon becomes chronically inflamed because of the diminished space through which the tendon travels. While impingement syndromes are generally thought of as a shoulder problem, they also occur in the ankle. Impingements commonly occur in the front of the ankle (anterior impingement) in male dancers who dance bravura roles. With time, this can cause bone spurs (osteophytes) to build up. These can cause pain, loose bodies (typically pieces of cartilage or bone that have broken loose and are floating around) and limitation of the plié. If the symptoms warrant, an anterior cleanout of the ankle may be necessary. The opposite: Posterior impingement can occur when a dancer has an extra bone, the os trigonum, in the back of the ankle. [See FIGURE 50.]

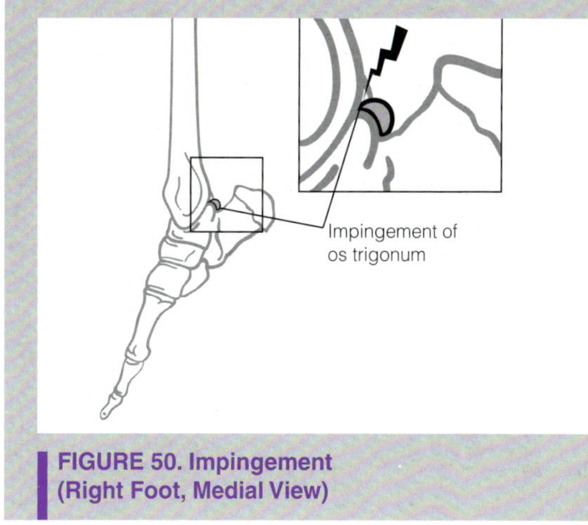

FIGURE 50. Impingement (Right Foot, Medial View)

Inversion: The inward movement of the heel and foot beneath the ankle, as when one sprains the outside of an ankle. [See FIGURE 13.]

J.

Jumper's knee: There is a short tendon in the knee that joins the kneecap (patella) to the upper shinbone (tibia) below, the patellar tendon. [See FIGURE 25.] It can be overloaded and develop tendonitis, especially in dancers and athletes who jump a lot. When injured, it hurts to jump, sit for long intervals or go down stairs. Jumper's knee can last a long time and be difficult to treat.

K.

Kyphosis: The opposite of lordosis. It is a forward bending or "hunchback" deformity usually found in the thoracic spine. [See FIGURE 45.]

L.

Labral tears of the hip: The hip socket has a cartilaginous lip (labrum) that is thought to add depth to the socket. This labrum can be torn either by an acute injury or by forcing turnout. It causes pain and snapping in the groin that is often mistaken for iliopsoas tendonitis. These labral tears may sometimes require arthroscopic surgery if they don't respond to rest and physical therapy. [See FIGURE 39.]

Lateral: Pertaining to the outside, or toward the outside of the body. The opposite of lateral is medial.

Leg pain: Pain in the lower leg can be due to one of three things: shin splints, a compartment syndrome or stress fractures. At times it can be hard to tell the difference. Shin splints can occur anteriorly and posteriorly. Anterior shin splints usually cause pain over a two- to three-inch area where a muscle attaches to the shinbone. The pain is aggravated when increasing speed and distance when running. Compartment syndromes cause a more generalized leg pain that increases with sustained activity such as running. They are relatively rare in dancers, whose activities are more episodic than continuous. Stress fractures are activity-related, but are very localized, often with a small tender bump on the bone. You can usually locate them with one finger. A bone scan will detect them early.

Lordosis: An increase in the swayback of the lower spine. [See FIGURE 45.] Lordosis may be associated with poor posture, birth defects, neuromuscular problems, back surgery or a hip problem. It is often seen in young dancers who hope to increase their turnout. It is a bad habit and should be discouraged.

M.

Malalignment: Pain around the patella is occasionally a sign that the patella is not aligned properly and may be tracking off-center (typically toward the outside). Patellar malalignment is very common in female athletes because their hips are placed farther apart for child-bearing. Accordingly, the knees come together below, so there is a natural valgus (knock-knee). [See FIGURE 40.] In sports medicine, malalignment has been referred to as “the miserable or malicious malalignment syndrome.”

Medial: Pertaining to the middle, or toward the middle of the body. Medial is the opposite of lateral. For example, the medial side of the knee is the side closest to the other knee, whereas the lateral side of the knee is the outside of the knee.

Meniscus: These are two crescent-shaped cartilaginous shock absorbers inside the knee, one on the inside (medial), the other on the outside (lateral). They can be torn, usually with a twisting or bending injury, which causes pain, swelling and catching in the knee. If the symptoms warrant, the problem can usually be successfully managed with arthroscopic surgery. [See FIGURE 27.]

Morton’s neuroma: A thickened nerve in the foot, usually between the third and fourth toes. The most common complaints include pain, unusual sensations and numbness in the fore foot corresponding to the toes adjacent to the neuroma. The pain is described as sharp and burning, and it may be associated with cramping. It has been suggested that it may, in part, be caused by wearing tight shoes. It is no more common in ballet dancers than in non-dancers.

MRI (Magnetic Resonance Imaging): A special radiology examination usually done when it is important to see both soft tissue (e.g., tendons and ligaments) and bone detail. It does not involve the use of X-rays. If the primary interest is in the bone, a CT scan may be preferable. These exams are so sensitive that they may reveal abnormalities that don’t have anything to do with the presenting problem, so it is very important to correlate the findings with the history and physical examination.

MRSA: An infection caused by a strain of Staphylococcus aureus bacteria that is resistant to antibiotics known as beta-lactams. These antibiotics include methicillin, amoxicillin and penicillin. MRSA infections can present as a cellulitis, sty, boil or an abscess.

N.

NSAIDs: Anti-inflammatory medicines, such as ibuprofen, used and misused in the treatment of injuries. Unfortunately, they are often given as a quick way to relieve pain without adequate consideration of the condition that is causing the pain. They should be used as part of an overall treatment program that includes modified activity and physical therapy. They should rarely, if ever, be given to children under the age of 12, and they should not be given to anyone allergic to aspirin. There is evidence that NSAIDs may slow bone and tendon healing.

O.

Orthopedist or Orthopedic Surgeon: A Medical Doctor (MD) or a Doctor of Osteopathy (DO) who has had specialty training in injuries and disorders of the musculoskeletal system.

Osgood Schlatter's disease, or "choir boy's knee": This is the adolescent's version of the "jumper's knee," but instead of straining the patellar tendon, the injury occurs in the growth plate of the bone where the tendon attaches to the bone (tibial tubercle) below the knee. The area overlying the tubercle becomes sore and swollen, but heals with rest. [See FIGURE 42.]

Osteopenia: The term used for bones that have become somewhat less dense than normal, but not as severe as in osteoporosis.

Os trigonum: The second most common extra bone in the foot after the accessory navicular bone. It occurs in 8-10 percent of people with a 50 percent incidence of being present in both feet. It lies in the back of the ankle and can limit the pointe position on relevé and may or may not be painful. Many dancers have this bone and have no trouble with it. Others have persistent symptoms and may need to have it removed. [See FIGURE 37.]

P.

Physical therapy (PT): The hallmark of the conservative treatment of dance injuries, preferably by a therapist with supplemental training in dance injuries and rehabilitation.

Podiatrist: A foot doctor who attended Podiatry School (not medical school) and who may or may not have additional training in dance. They may be confused with Medical Doctors or Osteopathic Doctors.

Posterior: The back of the body or body part.

Pronation: The rolling in or lowering of the inner (medial) side of the foot so that the arch is lowered or flattened. The opposite motion is supination.

Proprioception: The ability to sense the position, location, orientation and movement of the body and its parts.

Q.

R.

Retroversion: The opposite of anteversion. People who have this are "duck-footed," meaning that they are naturally turned out. Because it enables greater turnout, retroversion is more desirable in dancers.

S.

Scoliosis: A sideways curve of the spine that occurs primarily in young females 10-16 years of age. [See FIGURE 46.] Most scoliosis is thought to be inherited and is not caused by muscle imbalance, leg length inequalities or by carrying heavy book bags. Its course is unpredictable; some progress steadily while others don't, so those with scoliosis need to be followed very carefully. The hallmark of treatment is early detection of progressive curves and bracing. Ballet class, which helps maintain flexibility and strength, is thought to be a good part of the treatment program.

Sesamoids: Two small bones inside of tendons, similar to miniature kneecaps, that lie under the head of the first metatarsal bone (in the ball of the foot just beneath the big toe joint). [See FIGURE 4.] Most of the time they produce no symptoms, but occasionally they cause pain; they can fracture either by a direct blow or from stress. They often heal slowly and, for reasons that are unknown, can die due to a loss of blood supply, rather than heal (avascular necrosis). If they fail to heal they may need to be removed.

Shin splints: Pain in the front of the lower leg where muscles attach to the shinbone (tibia). (See "Leg pain.")

Spine: The spine is anatomically divided into four parts: the cervical spine in the neck; the dorsal or thoracic spine in the chest area; the lumbar spine in the lower back; and the sacrum at the back of the pelvis. [See FIGURE 32.]

Spondylolisthesis: If a spondylolysis (see below) occurs on both sides of the lower back it can weaken the attachment between the vertebrae and allow one vertebra to slip forward on the adjacent vertebra. This slippage is called a spondylolisthesis. It commonly occurs in dancers and gymnasts. [See FIGURE 52.]

Spondylolysis: A defect, like a stress fracture, in the lower spine where the lumbar spine joins the pelvis. It usually happens on one side or the other and is characterized by pain in grand battement derrière on the affected leg but not the other. The defect can usually be discerned on a bone scan or MRI study. [See FIGURE 51.]

Sprain: An injury to a ligament. Sprains are usually classified as mild, moderate or severe (Grade I, II or III) depending upon the severity of the injury. [See FIGURE 34.]

Strain: An injury to a muscle or a tendon, not a ligament. Strains, like sprains, are also graded, as are most injuries, as mild, moderate or severe. [See FIGURE 35.]

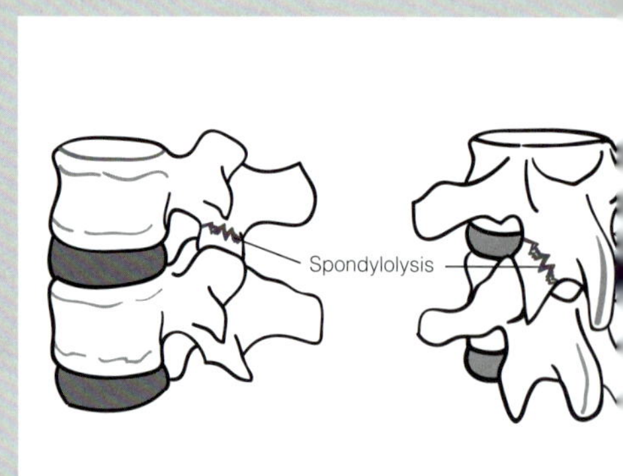

FIGURE 51. Spondylolysis

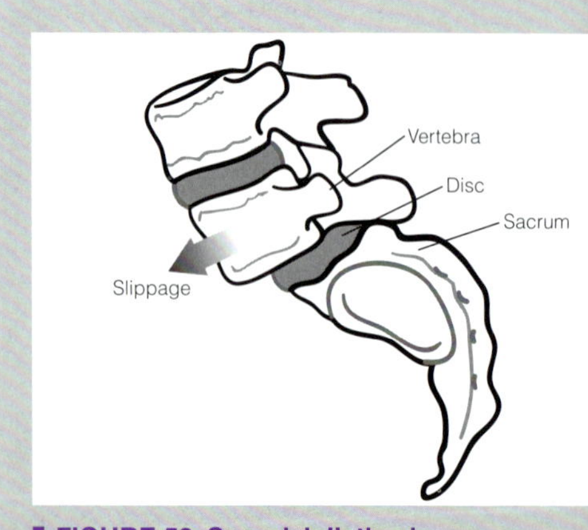

FIGURE 52. Spondylolisthesis

Stress fracture: A micro-fracture in a bone caused by repetitive overload, similar to bending a paper clip until it snaps. These are frequently seen in the feet of female dancers and the shins of male dancers. They are particularly common in females who don't menstruate properly or have poor nutrition or an eating disorder (see Part 2 for more on nutrition and eating disorders). There is a particular type of stress fracture usually seen in the tibia of male dancers that can go unrecognized for months. This injury is associated with a characteristic picture on the X-ray referred to as the "Dreaded Black Line." Because blood supply to the area is poor, tibial stress fractures are extremely slow to heal.

Stress reaction: Similar to a stress fracture but not as severe. It is akin to repeatedly bending a paper clip that hasn't broken yet.

Subluxation: Refers to a partial dislocation of a joint.

Subtalar joint: The joint beneath the true ankle joint. It consists of the talus on top and calcaneus on the bottom. The subtalar joint is responsible for the side-to-side motion of the heel that enables the foot to turn in and out (inversion and eversion). [See FIGURES 13 and 14.]

Supination: Refers to turning inward, for example, the turning inward of the foot so that the bottom faces inward. Supination is the opposite of pronation.

Synchondrosis: Refers to a type of cartilaginous joint that is temporary and exists during the growing phase. It becomes progressively thinner during skeletal maturation, ultimately becoming obliterated, as in the closure of the epiphyses.

Syndesmosis: A joint in which the bones are united by fibrous connective tissue forming an interosseus membrane or ligament that allows a modest amount of movement. [See FIGURE 9.]

T.

Talus: The bone of the ankle that articulates with the tibia and fibula above to form the true ankle joint, and the calcaneus below to form the subtalar joint. [See FIGURES 13 and 14.]

Tendonitis: Refers to the inflammation of a tendon usually due to microscopic damage from overload. The tendon becomes swollen and painful. A vicious cycle of increasing swelling and pain may occur. Because the tendon is swollen, it binds as it moves in the surrounding tissues and the binding causes the tendon to become even more inflamed and swollen. The treatment is usually ice, reduced use of the affected body part and physical therapy. Although the condition is frequently due to unrecognized tightness in the muscle-tendon unit, stretching should not be done while the tendon is healing. Premature stretching of an inflamed tendon will make the tendon heal more slowly. Stretching should be done only after the tendon is completely healed to prevent recurrence of the problem. NSAIDs are frequently used in the management of tendonitis.

Tibia: The shinbone. It is a common location for stress fractures in male dancers. (See "Leg pain.") [See FIGURES 9 and 14.]

Turnout: The sum of the external rotation present in the hip plus the turnout below the knee. There is great variation in these components; many dancers have mediocre turnout in the hips, but manage to close in fifth position by gaining their rotation below the knee, which places a lot of stress on the knee. Some dancers have excellent turnout in the hip but actually lose some of it below the knee. Turnout can also vary greatly between the right and left sides in the same individual.

U.

V.

Valgum: See "Genu valgum."

Varum: See "Genu varum."

W.

X.

Y.

Z.

ABT

American Ballet Theatre

National Training Curriculum

Health: Part 2

DEVELOPMENT AND HEALTH

PART 2 CONTRIBUTING AUTHORS

Priscilla M. Clarkson, PhD

Virginia Wilmerding, PhD

Gary I. Wadler, MD, FACP, FACSM, FACPM, FCP

Caroline Silby, PhD, MEd

Lisa R. Callahan, MD

Lyle J. Micheli, MD

For the thousands of teachers who choose to devote themselves to the world of dance, there are hundreds of issues with which they will be confronted. At every turn, teachers are faced with critical decisions. There are many risks involved at all levels of dance training, including injuries, burnout, poor eating habits, dropout and even drug abuse. Yet, there are also wonderful opportunities to enhance and enrich the lives of young people. Balancing the development of a pre-professional dancer with the development of a child is not an easy task. The surest way to achieve this balance is for teachers to educate themselves about the numerous physical and psychological factors that impact dancers' development.

By gaining an understanding and awareness of these many factors, teachers will be better equipped to mitigate the pitfalls and pressures associated with dance involvement while also using dance as a way to enhance the life of a developing child.

American Ballet Theatre's Guidelines for Dancer Health examines some of the physical and psychological issues that affect dance students. This section of the curriculum is intended to be a resource for instructors as they define their teaching philosophies and structure their teaching environment. By making use of the following information, dance teachers have the opportunity to maximize the vast benefits dance participation can bring to a young person's life.

CHAPTER 8: Motor Control and Learning

INTRODUCTION

Movement is a fundamental function of living beings. The term "motor learning" refers to a permanent change in motor or movement performance. For example: A 10-year-old dancer comes to class knowing how to skip, but landing from a jump softly, carefully, consistently and with good performance quality is the result of motor learning. A dance teacher seeks to support these advancements in class. The more fully informed teachers are with regards to the various ways individuals learn, the more effective their teaching can be.

Learning a dance skill involves multiple steps: Material is presented by the teacher, replicated by the student and encoded in the student's mind. Given appropriate repetition, it is then stored in the student's long-term memory. To retrieve a memory, the student must first recall the step intellectually and then transfer the knowledge into the physical body. (When the intellectual recall is no longer necessary and the movement is reflexive in nature, this is referred to as "muscle memory.") Teachers assist in this process in two specific ways. They label the skills (for example: tendu, degagé, rond de jambe) and they teach movement relationships (for example: the grand battement gesture initiates a grand jeté). Once a student performs a step or sequence of steps, the teacher must be able to analyze his/her performance and provide feedback to further enhance motor learning and performance.

Note: The dancer recalls movement in two ways: overtly (physically) and covertly (cognitively). There is evidence to support the theory that covert rehearsal is as important as overt rehearsal. In other words, teachers should emphasize mental rehearsal—for instance going over choreography while lying in bed with your eyes closed—as an equally effective tool in dance sequence recall.

PERCEPTION

Motor learning begins with perception. Perception is a process of observing and organizing one's present experience and attaching meaning to it based on past experience.

Perception is...

- ...dependent on the senses (sight, touch, smell, hearing, taste).
- ...the process by which meaning is attached to information.
- ...modified by the learner's maturity, past experiences and motivation; the social and cultural context in which learning is taking place; and feedback from the teacher.

Perceptual skills

Perceptual skills include hand-eye coordination, rhythm, visual discrimination, spatial discrimination, body control and balance. Research indicates that these skills are not learned, but are genetically inherited. Building on and developing these innate skills is the very essence of ballet class. Each child brings to class a specific set of learning tools: his/her ability to stay "on task" (known as task persistence), personal sense of rhythm, preferred speed of moving and spatial preferences.

In ballet class, the teacher must be aware of the amount of information the student is receiving at one time. Some of it is relevant and some of it is not. For example: A teacher wants her students to think about how the movements relate to the music, not the temperature of the room or the color of her clothing. The teacher must use visual and verbal cues to focus the dancers' perception on the appropriate information. Directions must be short and to the point. Repetition of directions and step execution are key.

DEMONSTRATION AND MIMICKING

Motor learning begins with perception and continues with demonstration and mimicking.

In a traditional dance class, the teacher demonstrates a movement (the students perceive it) and then the students are asked to perform the movement. Lastly, the teacher provides verbal feedback to emphasize the motor development process.

As the class level increases, so do expectations from the teacher that students will be able to execute longer and more physically demanding dance combinations. But since all people learn in small chunks and are helped by focusing on specific points, dance teachers must make the most critical information prominent in the demonstration. Visual and verbal cues need to be specific and short. Clearly, a novice dancer will reach attention and information overload before an advanced dancer.

TEACHING METHODS

Learning a dance or movement skill is, in part, dependent upon how the information is presented. What is called "instructional cueing" can take three forms: verbal, visual and kinesthetic.

- **Verbal instruction** is the most common form of teaching, although it may not be the most effective when used alone. This form of instruction often dominates both technique and composition classes, with dance students spending up to two-thirds of a class listening to verbal instructions. Although it is an important part of motor learning, it should be used minimally. When verbal instruction is used in class, teachers can help students learn the vocabulary of ballet by emphasizing it.
- **Visual instruction** should accompany and complement verbal instruction. For example, a teacher or a more advanced dancer should demonstrate a movement, and then encourage students to try it. "Watching and doing" should be a predominant strategy in teaching.
- **Kinesthetic instruction** involves the actual execution of a dance skill and the perceptual awareness of the movement. This is known as proprioception. Proprioception involves a perception of sensations from the skin, joints, muscles and vestibular apparatus of the inner ears (providing balance). It is not enough to see and hear a dance sequence; effective learning requires the understanding of how the movement feels. Kinesthetic ability is of greater importance later in learning, when the mature learner can appreciate the integration of the movement, performance quality, musicality and the like. One way to encourage kinesthetic learning is to occasionally ask the dancers to face away from the mirror.

Kinesthetic instruction includes "hands-on" learning. It is not unusual in a dance class for the teacher to physically manipulate a student's limbs to get him/her to understand position and shape. This is an advanced method of teaching and should be used with discretion and an understanding of the individual's privacy. The current teaching atmosphere is such that issues of inappropriate touch and molestation are common points of concern and apprehension for teachers, students and their parents.

To use all three strategies and cue a dancer verbally, visually and kinesthetically, regardless of the dance form or level, would be the most effective method of enhancing motor learning. Dance sequences for the beginning dancer should emphasize visual and kinesthetic strategies. The advanced dancer can comprehend verbal instructions better. And keep in mind that "imaging," as educators call it, is equally as beneficial to learning as is moving. Using one's mind can save wear and tear on one's body.

OTHER MOTOR LEARNING CONSIDERATIONS

- **Feedback:** As the student matures from recreational to pre-professional to professional, teachers should instill the capacity for "self-instruction." As dancers become more advanced in their movement capacity, teachers should begin coaching the detailed idiosyncratic elements of each movement (tilt of the head, timing, dynamics).
- **Goal-setting:** Research has shown that establishing and explaining goals for both the short term (class) and long term (month or season) is also an effective and efficient teaching tool in the motor learning process. For example: A teacher can state that the goal of a given period of time will be piqué turns, and then each exercise that is planned to develop that movement would be pointed out. The teacher would identify how each choice for barre and center combinations supports that goal.

- **Motivation:** This is key in skill acquisition. Some research suggests that performance-oriented climates are linked to unproductive or negative behaviors (like the damaging effects of neurotic perfectionism—the obsessive drive to be perfect) that can actually interfere with learning and performance. Thus, in addition to setting goals for dance class, the teacher should provide a positive atmosphere that will be conducive to learning.
- **Repetition:** One cannot consider motor learning without considering the value of repetition. Once the appropriate neurological pattern is set up (and the movement is being executed correctly and efficiently), repetition will ingrain the skill into the body, in much the same way as walking on the neighbor's perfect yard will wear a path through it.
- **Cognitive behaviors:** Teachers of dance must understand that each dancer comes to them with different cognitive behaviors. This is commonly referred to as "multiple intelligences." Howard Gardner, a psychologist from Harvard Graduate School of Education, has outlined eight intelligences. They are:
    - Linguistic: the use of words, spoken or written
    - Logical-mathematical: reason, abstractions, numerical skills
    - Spatial: vision and understanding of how objects occupy space
    - Musical: rhythmic sense, musical pitch, composition ability
    - Kinesthetic: movement ability and the body
    - Interpersonal: the ability to learn and interact with others, usually extroverts, works best with others
    - Intrapersonal: usually introverts, one who works best alone
    - Naturalist: aware of personal goals and motivations

The question for the teacher is not, "How smart is each student?", but rather, "How is each student smart?" The aim must be to find how a student learns, and within the scope of a traditional class, teach to these individual strengths. This means emphasizing rhythm to one student, spatial properties to another and how the movement feels to yet another.

QUESTIONING TRADITION

Ballet technique class is embedded with tradition, but what we know today is that some implicitly accepted practices may not help the young dancer with skill acquisition. An oft-cited example of this concept is the traditional start of a ballet class—the grand plié. It is customary to begin class with this skill even though we know of its potential harmful effects on the knees. Also, in the interest of time, many ballet teachers discuss and demonstrate a dance sequence only to one side, usually the right. The assumption that very young students can learn the other side without assistance should be questioned.

- Motor learning as it relates to dance involves the concept of transfer of information. The ballet dancer practices skills at the barre that are repeated in the center. However, it has been suggested that this transfer of information does not occur as dance teachers may expect. Barre work prepares the gesture leg for center work, but might not prepare the standing leg adequately.

- It has also long been presumed that ballet class promotes even development of the right and left sides of the body. However, recent research on lateral bias indicates that the right and left sides of the body are not trained as symmetrically as one would presume. The right side is often the side that teachers and students use to demonstrate and mark combinations. The number of repetitions of an exercise on the left side of the body is substantially less in most ballet classes of all levels.

Although motor learning research continues to predominate in sports literature, dance researchers are just beginning to focus on motor learning for more effective classroom strategies. The goal is efficient and effective dissemination of the skills needed for the craft of dance, while instilling the understanding of dance as an art form. When assessed from a motor learning perspective, consistency in movement patterns should be the foundation of effective teaching.

CHAPTER 9: Phases of Development

INTRODUCTION

Teachers play a vital role in the physical and emotional growth of young dancers, but many teachers underestimate the influence they have on their students' emotional development. During the teenage years especially, it's critical that adolescents have someone outside of their immediate family see them as talented and special. Gaining an understanding and awareness of a young person's emotional development is vital to building healthy relationships with your dancers. Dance teachers have chosen a profession that provides them with an incredible opportunity to enrich and empower the lives of young people. The dance teacher should pursue this awesome responsibility daily with intensity and integrity.

PRE-SCHOOL (1-5 YEARS OLD)

CHARACTERISTICS

The pre-school years are characterized by curiosity, assertiveness and the excitement generated from discovering new abilities. While children's communication skills begin to improve, they must also learn to grapple with limits, which can cause frustration. Pre-school-aged children think in an illogical and magical fashion with little ability to see things from another's perspective. Their attention span is quite limited.

ROLE OF THE TEACHER

Children at this stage of development tend to mimic the adult world, so the main teaching tool for this age group is imitation. Children from 1-5 can't learn to dance from verbal instruction – they need to be able to watch and imitate their teachers. Numerous repetitions of the same movement pattern to achieve "correctness" are not recommended. Instead, provide opportunities for many varied movement experiences.

The dance teacher's main task here is to make class fun and keep things simple. Encourage children to explore new ways to move their bodies. Be sure to share in the fun, keeping in mind that the primary reason children participate in dance is to enjoy themselves, improve skills and be with friends. Keep classes short, show enthusiasm and reward effort.

ROLE OF THE PARENTS

Setting consistent and clear limits helps to maintain the child's safety and teach appropriate and acceptable behavior. These limits will provide the foundation for the autonomy that will emerge in later years. Encourage each child's attempt to become separate, and share in his/her fun.

PRE-ADOLESCENT (6-10 YEARS OLD)

CHARACTERISTICS

As children enter the early years of school, language capabilities improve—they can use words to help express their feelings and thoughts. They learn to control their physical movements, and logical thinking also emerges—they can understand cause and effect, better see the viewpoints of others and differentiate between more important pieces of information. They are often obsessed with the notion of fairness. You may hear complaints like, "It's not fair. You didn't yell at Sally for being late," or "Why do I have to do the turns again? You didn't make anyone else do it." Teachers will notice social changes as well. Girls tend to develop a "best friend," whereas boys may have six or seven more casual friends. The primary task for pre-adolescent children is to exert control over their environment. In order to do so, they must be provided ample opportunities to feel successful physically, socially and cognitively.

ROLE OF THE TEACHER

Emphasis needs to be on a dancer's process, not just the outcome. Much attention should be given to the controllable aspects of performance, such as effort, risk-taking, perceptions, goals and pre-performance routines. During this stage of development, teachers can help dancers learn to think about their performances. Encourage them to gain awareness of the effective and ineffective ways they think throughout a class. Pre-adolescent dancers need to begin processing how certain actions (thoughts, body language, breathing, etc.) contribute to specific outcomes (correct technique, improved performance, quicker turns, etc.).

Telling pre-adolescent dancers how to do something is simply not good enough. Teachers must provide strategies to help dancers grasp technical concepts. Teachers may have to demonstrate a movement or create a way for the dancer to remember a specific correction. For example, when trying to get a dancer to turn at a particular spot on the stage at a particular time in the music, direct the dancer to count the number of steps that lead into the turn instead of just telling him/her to "get there on time." Other strategies may include: key thoughts, refocusing exercises, breaking the skill down, doing a walk-through of the movement, drawing the movement, analyzing video and comparing a correction to a simple movement ("Bring your knees up as if you are stepping up a step").

It is the teacher's job to be a role model for how s/he wants students to present themselves, communicate, respond to stress and handle conflict and loss. This is a good time to set boundaries with parents by informing them of plans and expectations while also working together to iron out logistics, finances and roles. And don't forget to make dancing fun!

ROLE OF THE PARENT

The role of the parent is to provide descriptive feedback. The parents should reward their child for the skills s/he used to create a successful outcome: for example, saying, "Good job. I saw that you were frustrated, but you took a deep breath and refocused." When parents catch their children doing something right, they should tell them. They should focus on skill improvement and taking steps to move forward.

EARLY ADOLESCENCE (11-14 YEARS OLD)

CHARACTERISTICS

By early adolescence, teenagers are able to speculate about what they might be able to accomplish as adults. They can also sustain attention, better control impulses and process thoughts. The major developmental task is struggling to forge an identity while also wanting to be a part of the group. Issues about sexual identity may also emerge. Teenagers scrutinize their immediate family's values, beliefs and traditions. In their search for an identity, teenagers begin idolizing adult role models outside of their immediate family. As teachers, you are at the top of the idolization list.

Questions such as "Who do I want to be?" and "What do I want to do?" are of central concern. Teens are preoccupied with their appearance. They tend to compare themselves to their peers. They will assess the amount of time they put into dancing, their rate of improvement and their likelihood for future success. Not surprisingly, the highest dropout rate occurs during this stage of development.

Dance teachers should prepare themselves for their dancers to reconsider their commitment to dancing as they look to the future. These doubts are an appropriate part of a dancer's development and need to be addressed. Instead of scaring, guilting or threatening dancers into continued participation, discuss options, goals, training requirements, sacrifices and benefits of participation.

During this period of time, it can be easy for teachers to unknowingly undermine parents. Teenagers may complain to the teacher about their "crazy" parents. Take great care to validate the child's feelings without criticizing or attacking parental behavior.

Early adolescence marks the time when students must be reminded that success in dance is a process. At this stage, children may be devoting most of their time and energy to dance. Yet very few will live out their professional fantasy. Dancers drop out because fun turns to pressure or they believe they lack the physical capabilities to reach their goals. Regardless of dancers' talents, they all deserve to acquire the lessons and skills that you can bring to their lives.

ROLE OF THE TEACHER

This is the developmental stage where the teacher wants to focus on teaching dancers about the mental aspects of performance. Adolescents tend to feel self-conscious, especially girls. These insecurities are often coupled with increased anxiety and decreased performance levels. Be sure to reward effort, focus, goal-setting and small performance improvements. Provide opportunities for dancers to practice being under pressure as they are in performance. For example, pick one day a week that they must perform barre exercises, a combination or an entire dance for you and the class. Prior to their simulation, discuss some strategies (i.e., deep breathing, key thoughts and pre-performance routines) the dancers can use to ease anxiety and tension.

At this time, teenagers are searching for independence. Teachers should clearly communicate expectations, goals and teaching philosophies. Help teach strategies for dealing with performance anxiety and frustration from trying to master technique. Act as a sounding board and provide an open environment for dancers to communicate. Teachers should expect responsible behavior from their students at this age.

ROLE OF THE PARENT

Parents should set boundaries with and for their children. They should be role models for appropriate behavior, and teach coping strategies like deep breathing and refocusing. The focus should be on the process, not the outcome, of their child's endeavors. Parents can put situations—especially disappointments—into perspective without coaching or hovering over their child. They should provide an open opportunity for their child to communicate with them.

Note: The pressures of dance can be exacerbated by the onset of adolescence. It's not surprising that the highest dropout rate in dance occurs between the ages of 13 and 14. Adolescents experience dramatic decreases in self-esteem, are filled with self-doubt and are often consumed with pleasing other people. This can leave them feeling moody, self-critical and depressed.

MATURING ADOLESCENT (15-20 YEARS OLD)

CHARACTERISTICS

Once children have reached this stage of development, changes in cognitive abilities are minimal. However, the content of their cognitions changes significantly. They are questioning issues such as the "meaning of life" and religion. They are thinking about their communities as well as global and social issues. Other major concerns include uncertainty about the future, one's place in the world and separation from the immediate family. Dancers will likely struggle to balance academics, dance and social interactions. Helping dancers balance their lives serves to enhance their health and well-being and ultimately improves performance.

Physical changes may emerge, which in turn influence performance. Males are likely to show increases in their strength and speed while females may experience some difficulty adjusting to their new body size and composition following puberty.

ROLE OF THE TEACHER

At this stage of development, dancers will likely experience doubt about their capabilities and question their commitment to ballet. Allow their concerns to be heard and validated. Dancers at this age should be evaluating progress at appropriate points in time and with their teacher's assistance. To this end, some teachers find structured goal-setting and evaluation sessions helpful. Encourage dancers to think about performance and practice in a factual (not emotional) manner. (For example, "I need to work on my turnout" rather than "I have no turnout and I'll never reach my goals.") Teachers should listen to dancers' self-talk and discourage irrational thinking.

It is the dance teacher's job to help dancers balance life with dance. Recognize all aspects of each student's personality to nurture self-esteem. Allow dancer input. Create an open environment for dancers to communicate and help them keep things in perspective.

ROLE OF THE PARENT

Parents should be supportive. They should allow their child to drive some of the decisions s/he will be making. Parents should reframe disappointing situations, and not coach. They should create an open environment for their child to communicate with them.

CHAPTER 10: Psychological and Emotional Factors of Dance Training

INTRODUCTION

It has been said that parents have a better chance of winning a million dollars in the lottery than of watching their son or daughter become a professional ballet dancer. Placing too much pressure on a child can be potentially harmful. It can take years for a dancer to recover from the emotional damage caused by unrealistic expectations.

Regardless of achievement in the ballet studio, young people need to feel competent socially, intellectually, emotionally and physically. These competencies are the foundation from which self-esteem is developed. As dancers progress to higher levels of training, the choices they make will be driven by different factors than those of a lower-level dancer. For example, a lower-level dancer might choose to attend a summer sleep-away camp and forgo a few months of dance training or choose to participate in multiple activities rather than specializing only in dance. A pre-professional dancer, on the other hand, will place more focus on dance training, to the exclusion of other pursuits. The skills children require on the emotional side—regardless of their level of dance skill—remain the same. Even as dancers chart their path to the professional ranks, they will need assistance negotiating their emotional life.

In order to develop self-esteem through dance, the process of learning needs to be valued as much as performance outcomes. If the teacher places emphasis on the controllable aspects of performance (effort, focus, etc.), views mistakes as part of learning and encourages all talent levels, his/her students will experience less stress, more enjoyment and higher levels of self-esteem.

No matter what a dancer's physical abilities are, the teacher can assist him/her in developing certain emotional competencies. Here's how:

- Validate dancers' commitment to ballet. All children need to feel directed and productive. While progress may occasionally stall, their commitment to dance can be honored and respected.
- Allow dancers' voices to be heard. By listening, the teacher lets his/her students know that their thoughts are valid and worthy of being heard. The teacher may not necessarily agree with his/her students' opinions, but s/he can provide a safe environment in which students can learn to express themselves in a clear and appropriate way.
- Be a good role model for the use of effective coping skills. Validate dancers when they make use of refocusing, breathing, time-outs, etc. In order to excel, dancers will need to develop fairly advanced coping skills at a young age. Otherwise, they may end up dropping out.
- Emphasize to dancers the importance of balancing the opinion of others with what they know about themselves. Teach them to consider the opinions of those important to them along with their own ideas. This prevents them from rejecting useful information or becoming over-compliant.
- Reframe failures and mistakes as opportunities for learning. Teach dancers to process successful and unsuccessful performances in a productive manner.

The following observations have been made about girls who participate in sports, but many of the observations are also true of girls who participate in dance.

Girls who participate in sports have been shown to have higher self-esteem and do better in school. They are less likely to join gangs, do drugs or have unwanted pregnancies. Sports can empower girls and help them avoid some of the pitfalls of adolescence. Participating in sports enables them to see their bodies as the vessel that houses their many talents rather than just something that looks good. They learn to trust their capabilities and deal with errors and daily frustration. Girls can learn through sports that they are selected for a role based upon ability rather than popularity. Sports participation can instill character lessons such as perseverance, responsibility and commitment. Girls can develop mental skills such as goal-setting, focusing and imagery. Finally, they glean lessons about teamwork, friendships and communication. Regardless of achievement level, these are the life lessons that define the true value of sports participation.

PEER PRESSURE

Peer pressure is a term used to describe temptation or pressure from friends and peers to change actions, attitudes, morals and values. Individuals are expected to conform to the standards, expectations, outlooks, tastes and actions of the group. Peer pressure can affect drug and alcohol use, academic performance and choices in fashion, music, friends and boyfriends/girlfriends.

WHO DOES IT HAPPEN TO AND WHY?

Peer pressure is common during the transition from childhood to adolescence. Young people tend to act negatively toward individuals that are not members of their group or who show other physical or emotional differences. The following are traits that put people at higher risk of falling into the peer pressure trap:

- Low self-esteem
- Lack of confidence
- Uncertainty about one's place in the group
- Lack of interest outside the peer group
- Feeling isolated from peers/family
- Lack of direction in life
- Depression
- Eating disorders
- Drug and alcohol abuse
- Poor academic abilities
- Lack of strong ties to friends
- Close bond with a bully

WHAT'S THE EMOTIONAL AND PHYSICAL TOLL IT TAKES?

Peer pressure is often seen as negative as it usually refers to a young person being influenced to act in a manner that is harmful to him/herself or others. Yet, peer pressure can have a positive influence on behavior patterns, too, when an individual is connected to a group that values self-improvement, benevolence and achievement.

HOW CAN A TEACHER HELP PREVENT/ENCOURAGE IT?

Teachers can encourage positive peer pressure by having a "no tolerance" policy when it comes to bullying or acting with the intent to hurt another. Appreciate, recognize and reward dancers who show tolerance, patience and understanding of others. Provide opportunities for dancers to establish positive and strong relationships with their peers, to minimize the likelihood of negative peer influences.

Research has shown that teens with close ties to their parents are far less likely to become delinquent than students who feel distant from their families. Supportive parents and teachers provide a safe environment for children.

Ballet programs can encourage friendships and positive peer relationships in the early grades. Teachers need to make sure that grouping practices don't reinforce students' negative self-perceptions or derogatory labels of others. For example, avoid placing dancers in groups by body types. Instead, make sure that dancers within a group represent a range of body types and physical strengths. Additionally, schools can invite parents and other adult leadership to workshops that explain the dynamics of peer pressure.

Positive peer pressure

- Cheering on classmates
- Pushing classmates to do their best
- Encouraging focus

Negative peer pressure

- Discouraging classmates
- Interfering with classmates' progress
- Providing distractions

PRINT IT! THIS WORKSHEET CAN BE PRINTED AND PASSED OUT TO STUDENTS WHO MIGHT BE LEARNING TO DEAL WITH NEGATIVITY FROM PEERS.

TOOLS FOR HANDLING NEGATIVE COMMENTS FROM PEERS

1. Use Flattery

The problem: Your friend says something to you like, "This school stinks. The teachers are stupid and the kids are stuck-up."

The solution: Use flattery. Saying kind, thoughtful things about your friend often works to your advantage.

"You're too smart to really mean that."

"You usually have such nice things to say."

"You usually are so positive."

"You usually have such good ideas. What can we do to make things better?"

2. A Better Idea

The problem: Your friend says something to you like, "I think we should spread rumors about Sally via e-mail."

The solution: Quickly suggest something else to do or say—something better or kinder. Suggest an alternative with excitement and energy.

"Hey, I've got a good idea! Let's go..."

"Instead of talking behind Sally's back, let's go talk to her about it."

"This seems to be bothering you. Let's figure out a productive way to discuss it."

3. Return the Challenge

The problem: Your friend says something to you like, "You think you are so great just because you got the lead role. Don't you realize that nobody around here likes you?"

The solution: It is probably time to return the challenge and say:

"Friends don't gossip about one another."

"If you were my friend, you would focus on what you like about me."

"Friends talk directly to one another to resolve conflict."

4. Act Shocked

The problem: Your friend says something to you like, "You are so conceited. I hope they don't pick you for *The Nutcracker* tour."

The solution: Act amazed, as if you are in a state of shock! Look at your friend, let your mouth drop open, and say something like:

"I know you didn't mean that."

"I can't believe you even said that or suggested that."

"How silly!"

"I know you are a nice person, so you can't possibly mean that."

BURNOUT

Each year, numerous young people withdraw from dance participation. Some drop out to pursue new interests while others quit due to the extreme pressure they experience. Intense training demands coupled with high performance expectations and close adult supervision can induce feelings of stress, unhappiness and anxiety, and eventually lead to burnout.

WHAT IS IT?

Burnout is a state of emotional and physical exhaustion associated with frequent and ineffective attempts to meet practice and performance demands and expectations. It usually involves psychological, emotional and physical withdrawal from a formerly enjoyable activity, but it is complex and affects many aspects of life. Once a person is burned out, withdrawal from the environment causing the burnout is inevitable. Dancers who are burned out may feel hopeless, helpless, cynical, angry and out of control.

There are three terms that are used to describe the process of burnout. While these terms are used interchangeably, they are independent concepts.

- **Overtraining:** This occurs when dancers are practicing excessively and at maximal capacity for short periods of time (for example, three weeks), or when there is a marked increase in the intensity and frequency of their practices.
- **Staleness:** A physiological state of overtraining which manifests itself as deteriorated performance readiness. Staleness is the end result of overtraining. The dancer who is stale will have difficulty maintaining standard training and achieving previous results. A stale dancer will have a reduction in performance (five percent or greater for an extended period of at least two weeks). About 80 percent of stale athletes—both male and female—are clinically depressed. It has also been shown that 5-15 percent of elite skiers suffered staleness each year.
- **Stress:** While burnout may be the result of unrelenting stress, they are not the same. Stressed people may feel overwhelmed by pressure and obligations, but they still have the sense that if they can get everything under control, they will feel better. People who are burned out feel a true sense of helplessness and have little hope of being able to make positive change in their lives. Stressed people tend to recognize factors contributing to the stress, while burnout takes months to develop so the contributing factors become muddled and difficult to discern (helpguide.org).

THE FOLLOWING CHART SHOWS THE DIFFERENCES BETWEEN STRESS AND BURNOUT.

Stress vs. Burnout

STRESS	**BURNOUT**
Characterized by over-engagement	Characterized by disengagement
Emotions are over-reactive	Emotions are blunted
Produces urgency and hyperactivity	Produces helplessness and hopelessness
Exhausts physical energy	Exhausts motivation and drive, ideals and hope
Leads to anxiety disorders	Leads to paranoia, detachment and depression
Causes disintegration	Causes demoralization
Primary damage is physical	Primary damage is emotional
Stress may "kill" you prematurely, and you won't be able to finish what you started.	Burnout may never "kill" you, but your life may not seem worth living.

WHO IS AT RISK FOR BURNOUT?

All dancers are at high risk for burnout. Understanding the risk factors can help dance teachers guide their students toward health and away from the pitfalls of burnout.

- **Logistical risk factors:** Ballet requires dancers to make social and academic sacrifices to accommodate the rigors associated with high-level training. Dancers may not have adequate time to devote to studies or other extra-curricular activities. Dancers can also experience social isolation, as they may attend school for fewer hours and have little social time to spend with their dancing peer group.
- **Emotional risk factors:** The pressure to consistently perform on and offstage at a high level can cause stress, and if attempts to meet demands are frequent and ineffective, burnout is inevitable. Teachers' and parents' inappropriate or unfulfilled expectations can contribute to the development of burnout. As expectations for performance increase and dancers become more outcome-focused, they often lose sight of and disconnect from the feelings of competence and satisfaction that dance brings to their lives. Driven and achievement-oriented dancers with high standards and intolerance for mistakes are especially at risk for burning out.

WHAT ARE THE SYMPTOMS?

Since burnout develops over time, it's critical to identify the early warning signs. Burnout has its roots in stress and an individual can experience physical, emotional, intellectual, social and spiritual symptoms.

Physical symptoms include:

- General fatigue or exhaustion at dance and at home
- Disordered sleep
- Sexual dysfunction
- Headaches
- Gastrointestinal discomfort

Intellectual symptoms include:

- Lowered ability to concentrate
- Short-term memory loss
- Little interest in trying new things
- A defeated and negative attitude about change
- Lack of interest in outside activities
- Viewing challenges as obstacles

Emotional symptoms include:

- Lack of positive emotions and feeling emotionally depleted, which can lead to illness
- Lack of optimism
- Little tolerance for mistakes and change
- Sarcasm, temper tantrums, emotional outbursts, withdrawal and low self-esteem
- Little interest or time for non-dance related activities

Social symptoms include:

- Social isolation
- Unwillingness to share emotions, especially ones that are seen as imperfect, such as anger, frustration, doubt, worry and/or loneliness
- Sharing is seen as a sign of weakness

Spiritual symptoms include:

- Loss of purpose for dancing
- Questioning of commitment to dance
- Failure to focus on process
- Focus on undesirable performance outcomes

PREVENTION

The best solution to burnout is prevention. Dance teachers can help prevent burnout by following these four simple suggestions:

- Consider the total length of the training season and pace dancers appropriately. Light rehearsals can be mixed with more intense classes. By adhering to cycles in training, referred to as periodization, teachers can ensure that their students' bodies have adequate time to recover from physical and emotional stress before any additional training is undertaken. Appropriate and realistic goal-setting can help guide dancers throughout the season and provide motivation and accountability.
- Be aware of external events that are occurring in a dancer's life, such as the start of school, final exams, divorce, remarriage, sibling stress, parent conflicts and family illness. These circumstances can have an influence on performance.
- Find creative ways to make training fun and interesting. For instance, make use of games, contests, challenges, rewards, group learning and variety. Monotony of training can lead to burnout.
- Recognize all aspects of a dancer's personality by providing time away from the studio for non-dance activities. Performance feedback should be balanced and focus on the process. Remind dancers to connect with how they want ballet to make them feel—for example, competent, satisfied, free, in-control and happy—and point out moments when they experience these emotions. Teachers can involve dancers in decision-making by soliciting their opinions, thoughts and feelings. Catch them doing something right and empower them to take charge of their emotions.

INTERVENTION

Once burnout has occurred, intervention is necessary. Recognition of burnout is key to beginning intervention. The following things can help a student return to health.

- **Redefine success:** As dancers pass through various stages of their development, they must be willing to redefine "success." Burned-out dancers typically feel as though they are not meeting their definition of success. By redefining "success," dancers can begin to place importance on the daily actions that move them closer to meeting their ultimate objectives, rather than solely focusing on their perceived failures.
- **Acknowledge progress:** Watching video of ballet accomplishments can help dancers to reconnect with their own success and progress. Videos highlighting one's progression over time can be especially powerful.
- **Rediscover love of dance:** Burned-out dancers often need to return to the basics to rediscover their love of dance. Some individuals find keeping a journal to be an enriching way to reconnect with their passion for dance. Talking with other dancers who have overcome burnout can also provide comfort.
- **See a psychologist:** Referral to a sports psychologist can assist dancers in sorting through their confusion, stress and worry. Having an objective person to hear a dancer's concerns and guide him/her through decision-making can be invaluable.

DROPOUT

Ultimately, if dancers cannot define a clear purpose for involvement in dance or develop strategies to cope with the stress of training, they will drop out. Many dancers will drop out when they perceive their capabilities to be inadequate to meet their goals. Still others will drop out due to lack of encouragement. This may be especially true for girls, for whom the dance environment tends to be highly competitive.

When it comes to sports, girls drop out at a higher rate than boys—some studies of athletes have shown dropout among girls to be six times greater! This may in part be attributed to the fact that during adolescence, girls show a dramatic decrease in self-esteem. Some studies cite as much as a 30-percent dropout rate. Adolescent girls are more likely to lose interest in activities that once challenged them, and are less likely to believe in their own abilities and less likely to question authority even when they believe the authorities are wrong. Girls worry about pleasing others and meeting external standards, which can leave them feeling critical, moody and depressed. Often, these issues stall not only athletic development, but emotional maturation as well. Yet, when the training environment is structured properly, sports (and perhaps dance) can help young women avoid some of these pitfalls of adolescence.

Male athletes tend to focus more on their desire to compete and win, while female athletes focus more on personal performance levels. Elite athletes must focus on both winning and on personal improvement.

FAST FACTS ABOUT ADOLESCENT GIRLS:

- Girls attribute failure to themselves.
- Girls look to have a personal relationship with their coach/instructor.
- Girls prefer coaches/instructors that communicate openly.
- Girls prefer coaches/instructors that are empathetic.
- Friendship and team unity are important to girls.
- Girls are sensitive to the thoughts and feelings of classmates and teammates.
- Girls prefer their confidence not to be attacked.
- Girls prefer receiving one chunk of information at a time.
- Girls are more productive in environments that focus on personal improvement.

FAST FACTS ABOUT ADOLESCENT BOYS:

- Boys need to separate from their parents earlier than girls.
- Boys frequently need more physical space and need to be the ones to initiate physical contact with their parents.
- Males tend to focus in on one task.
- Males' "fight or flight" response is more rapidly engaged.
- If involved in high school athletics, boys are more likely to get better grades and go to college.
- If involved in high school athletics, boys are more likely to drink and try drugs.
- Male athletes have a "win" orientation.

PERSONALITY CHARACTERISTICS OF OUTSTANDING ATHLETES, LIKELY TO BE SHARED BY DANCERS:

- More achievement-oriented
- More independent
- More aggressive
- More emotionally stable
- More assertive

SUBSTANCE ABUSE AND DANCE

Although drug abuse in sports dates back hundreds of years, it is only in recent years that it has become such a compelling issue. The dance world is not immune to the abuse of recreational and performance-enhancing drugs that has so undermined sports world wide.

WHY DOES IT HAPPEN?

Currently there is no known data substantiating the use of anabolic steroids or other performance-enhancing drugs by dancers. However, in the current climate of drug use, one can never totally dismiss the possibility that dancers are using drugs, whether they be performance-enhancing or social drugs. Like athletes, dancers are driven by the pursuit of excellence, and in that pursuit they may resort to substance abuse.

WHO IS AT RISK?

Although ballerinas may call upon the strength and power needed for sports such as baseball and track and field, the aesthetic component of a dancer's performance requires the maintenance of flexibility. Dancers need leanness and grace, whereas steroid use tends to add weight and physical bulk. However, at least theoretically, a male dancer could use steroids to gain the strength required for partnering.

It should be noted that not all performance-enhancing drugs are used for strength. The aesthetic component of ballet, particularly for the female dancer, can take on the form of the relentless pursuit of thinness. In the extreme, that may manifest as a severe eating disorder, which in athletics has been referred to as the female athlete triad (disordered eating, amenorrhea and osteoporosis). (For more on this, turn to page 70.) Part and parcel of that disorder is the abuse of weight-control drugs such as stimulants, diuretics and laxatives. These behaviors are known to occur in the related disciplines of gymnastics and figure skating.

DETECTING THE SYMPTOMS

Although the symptoms of drug abuse can be extremely subtle, particularly in fit and accomplished dancers, dance teachers may be in the best position to detect such abuse because they observe their students' appearance and behavior on a regular basis. Unexplained changes in physical appearance, behavior, mood, performance or concentration all may be symptoms of drug abuse.

BROACHING THE SUBJECT OF DRUG ABUSE

Perhaps one of the most difficult problems for a dance teacher is approaching a student suspected of abusing drugs. As an authority figure, the dance teacher must approach the student and/or family, depending on the student's age, with respect and in an appropriate and confidential setting. In so doing, the teacher should be aware of his/her own pre-existing attitudes, prejudices and insecurities regarding drug abuse. The teacher should be aware of and knowledgeable about resources that are available to assist him/her in directing the dance student toward professional help.

EATING DISORDERS

WHAT ARE THEY?

Because dance is associated with slim bodies, dancers can develop an obsession with having a low body weight. This obsession may lead to an eating disorder.

The two most common eating disorders are anorexia nervosa and bulimia nervosa. Anorexia nervosa is an eating disorder in which a person refuses to stay at even the minimum weight considered normal for his/her age and height. Anorexia nervosa is associated with an intense fear of gaining weight, a disturbance in body image (thinking one is fatter than one actually is), and amenorrhea (lack of a menstrual cycle) in girls. Bulimia nervosa is an illness defined by food binges, or recurrent episodes of significant overeating, that are accompanied by a sense of loss of control. In addition to the overeating, bulimia is associated with purging (vomiting, using laxatives or diuretics) to prevent weight gain. Bulimics may also suffer from anorexia nervosa. These eating disorders are serious and can even result in death if not treated.

Note: Unfortunately, not all bodies are naturally suited for a career in ballet, an art form which often rewards high arches, long limbs and flexible joints. It is important that teachers and parents not place unrealistic goals for a professional career on a dance student whose body is limiting. This pressure can lead to injuries, low self-esteem, eating disorders, unhappiness and frustration.

WHO IS AT RISK?

The incidence of eating disorders is higher in girls; less than 10 percent of eating disorders occur in men and boys. Eating disorders generally start at or above age 13, but there have been cases reported in younger children.

Pre professional and professional dancers, especially girls, are at increased risk for an eating disorder because of their age, the thin aesthetic (the lean body shape) that is associated with dance and the stress associated with achieving success.

While both pre-professional and recreational dancers, especially girls, are at an increased risk of an eating disorder compared to the general public, the recreational dancer does not have the same performance pressures and is therefore likely to be less at risk than a pre-professional dancer.

THE EMOTIONAL AND PHYSICAL TOLL AN EATING DISORDER CAN TAKE

Low food intake can result in loss of muscle mass, fatigue, injury and illness. Low caloric intake can also lead to disruption of reproductive function in female dancers, specifically cessation of periods (amenorrhea). Dancers must be encouraged to eat sufficient food to provide the necessary energy for performance. Emphasis on low body weight or low body fat may benefit performance only if the guidelines are realistic, the calorie intake is reasonable and the diet is nutritionally sound (sample guidelines are provided in the nutrition section of this document). The use of extreme weight-control measures can jeopardize health and trigger behaviors associated with the eating disorders anorexia nervosa and bulimia nervosa.

In the extreme, these eating disorders can lead to semi-starvation, dehydration and even death.

WHAT ARE THE WARNING SIGNS?

Anorexia nervosa: Drastic loss of weight; a preoccupation with food, calories and weight; preoccupation with appearance; wearing baggy or layered clothing; relentless, excessive exercise; mood swings; and avoiding food-related social activities.

Bulimia nervosa: Recurring binge eating, usually followed by some method of purging, such as vomiting, diuretic or laxative abuse, or intense exercise.

General warning signs: Excessive concern about weight, change in physical appearance, bathroom visits after meals, depressive moods, strict dieting followed by eating binges, and increasing criticism of one's body.

It is important to note that the presence of one or two of these warning signs does not necessarily indicate the presence of an eating disorder, but may indicate a sub-clinical form of disordered eating. A definitive diagnosis should be made by appropriate health professionals.

WHY DOES IT HAPPEN?

Eating disorders are often an expression of underlying emotional distress that may have developed long before the individual was involved in dance. It has been suggested that stress, whether it be from participating in dance, striving for academic success or pursuing social relationships, may trigger eating disorders in susceptible individuals. Eating disorders can be triggered in such individuals by a single event or comments from a person important to the individual. In dance performance, such triggering mechanisms may include offhand remarks about appearance or constant badgering about a dancer's weight, body composition or body type.

PREVENTIVE MEASURES AND PRECAUTIONS

Decisions regarding weight loss should be based on the following recommendations, to reduce the potential of an eating disorder:

- Discourage frequent weigh-ins (either as a class or individually).
- Any discussions or recommendations regarding weight or percentage of body fat should be left to the dancer's physician or nutritionist, particularly during the teenage years.
- A responsible and realistic weight loss plan should be developed on an individual basis in concert with the dancer's physician and parents.

For each dancer, there may be a unique optimal body composition for performance, for health and for self-esteem. However, in most cases, these three values are not identical. Mental and physical health should not be sacrificed for performance. An erratic or lost menstrual cycle, sluggishness or an obsession with achieving a number on a scale may be signs that health is being challenged.

FEMALE ATHLETE TRIAD

Some girls who play sports, dance or exercise intensely are at risk of developing a disorder referred to as the female athlete triad. The triad is a combination of low energy availability (not ingesting sufficient food to match energy needed for dance exercise), amenorrhea (loss of periods) and osteoporosis (a thinning and weakening of the bones). Low energy availability can occur with or without an eating disorder. The low levels of estrogen associated with low energy availability and excessive exercise contribute to menstrual irregularities and thinning of the bones. If a dancer is suspected of having the triad, or even one or two components of the triad, she should be referred to her primary care physician for appropriate diagnosis and management.

In 2007, the American College of Sports Medicine, in a position stand, called for all individuals working with physically active girls and women to be educated about the female athlete triad and to develop plans for prevention, recognition, treatment and risk reduction. The position stand recommended that:

- Screening for the triad should occur at a pre-participation examination or annual health screening.
- Dancers with one component of the triad should be assessed for others.
- Dancers with disordered eating should be referred to a mental health practitioner for evaluation, diagnosis and recommendations for treatment.
- A test of bone mineral density should be done after a stress or low-impact fracture and after a total of six months of amenorrhea, menstrual cycle irregularity or disordered eating.
- Multidisciplinary treatment for the triad disorders should include a physician (or other health care professional), a registered dietitian and, for dancers with disordered eating, a mental health practitioner.
- Emphasis should be placed on optimizing energy availability and care should be taken to ingest sufficient calcium and Vitamin D in the diet to build and maintain bones.

OTHER RECOMMENDATIONS:

- Teachers should avoid pressuring female dancers to diet and lose weight and should be educated about the warning signs of eating disorders.
- Dancers should be educated about proper nutrition, safe training practices and the risks and warning signs of the female athlete triad.

SOME SIGNS AND SYMPTOMS OF THE FEMALE ATHLETE TRIAD:

- Weight loss
- Absent or irregular periods
- Stress fractures
- Muscle injuries
- Excessive fatigue
- Frequent trips to the bathroom, particularly after eating
- Preoccupation with food and weight
- Brittle hair and nails

MENSTRUAL CYCLE

FAST FACTS:

- The onset of menses, known as menarche, typically occurs anywhere from 9-16 years of age.
- The typical "normal" menstrual cycle can vary from 23-35 days, with an average of 28 days.
- A girl is considered to have primary amenorrhea (lack of normal menses) if she has not begun to menstruate by age 16.
- If she begins to menstruate, but then stops having menstrual periods, she is considered to have secondary amenorrhea.
- Amenorrhea is generally defined as lack of menses for at least 3 months.
- Oligomenorrhea refers to a menstrual cycle that occurs inconsistently, irregularly and at longer intervals. It is typically defined as three to six menstrual cycles per year, or cycles lasting longer than 38 days.
- Menstrual cycle irregularities are often accompanied by low levels of estrogen, known as hypoestrogenemia.
- Girls who take more than 12-14 hours of dance classes per week often experience a delayed onset of menarche.

Surveys regarding the prevalence of menstrual-cycle irregularities are not consistently reliable, as the definition of menstrual function can vary depending on how the survey was conducted. However, menstrual cycle irregularities are considered common in athletic populations, and have been reported in 15-60 percent of exercising women. These changes may be normal physiologic adaptations to exercise, or they may be an underlying medical problem.

While there are several possible medical causes of menstrual irregularities (such as thyroid and ovarian disorders), much of the current research in female athletes has focused on the relationship between energy expenditure from exercise and energy intake from the diet.

WHAT ARE THE POTENTIAL CONSEQUENCES OF MENSTRUAL IRREGULARITIES?

- Infertility: Although one oft-cited concern is infertility, fortunately, the long-term effects of menstrual cycle dysfunction on fertility appear to be reversible.
- Skeletal demineralization: A more immediate concern for both the adolescent and young adult female is skeletal demineralization, which occurs in hypoestrogenic women. Skeletal demineralization (decreased calcium) was first observed in amenorrheic athletes in 1984. Initially, the lumbar spine appeared to be the primary site where skeletal demineralization occurred, but new techniques for measuring bone mineral density now show that demineralization occurs throughout the skeleton. The loss of bone mass during prolonged hypoestrogenemia (low estrogen) is not completely reversible. Therefore, young women with low levels of circulating estrogen due to menstrual irregularities are at risk for low peak bone mass, which may increase the potential for osteoporotic fractures. An increased incidence of stress fractures also has been observed in the long bones and feet of women with menstrual irregularities.

TREATING MENSTRUAL IRREGULARITIES

The treatment goal for women with menstrual irregularities is the re-establishment of an appropriate hormonal environment for the maintenance of bone health. This can be achieved by normalizing one's caloric intake and energy expenditure or by hormone-replacement therapy, although it is critical to realize that neither has been shown to result in complete recovery of the lost bone mass. Although treating menstrual irregularities with oral contraceptives may restore the menstrual cycle, there is no evidence that this popular practice has a positive effect on bone mass. Therefore, it is imperative to recognize menstrual irregularities as possibly representing a hypoestrogenic state, and each young woman with such a condition should be thoroughly evaluated. Additional research is necessary to develop a specific prognosis for exercise-induced menstrual dysfunction.

All student-athletes with menstrual irregularities should be seen by a physician. General guidelines include:

1. Full medical evaluation, including an endocrine evaluation. Depending on age, a bone mineral density test should be considered. (There is more consistent normative data for those 18 years of age and older.)
2. Nutritional counseling with specific emphasis on:
    a. Total caloric intake versus energy expenditure.
    b. Adequate calcium intake of 1,200 to 1,500 milligrams a day.
    c. Adequate amounts of other nutrients critical to bone health–especially Vitamin D.
3. Continued monitoring of the diet, menstrual function and exercise schedule. All forms of exercise, including weight training and flexibility training, should be part of a healthy regimen.

Only if menstrual cycles are not satisfactorily restored with these measures should estrogen-progesterone supplementation be considered. This should be coupled with appropriate counseling on hormone replacement, review of family history and continued monitoring. Hormone-replacement therapy is thought to be important for amenorrheic women and oligomenorrheic women whose hormonal profile reveals an estrogen deficiency.

CHAPTER 11: Creating a Healthy Training Environment

INTRODUCTION

Motivation is the desire and willingness to act. A dancer's personality influences motivation levels, as do the environments in which s/he trains. One of the most challenging parts of a teacher's job is creating a training environment that facilitates the development of dancers with diverse motives for dancing. Research has identified two types of training environments:

- **Task-Involving Climate:** The "task-involving climate" is one in which teachers encourage collaborative learning, view mistakes as part of the learning process, value every dancer's contributions (not just those of the most talented) and place great emphasis on effort, use of positive self-talk and refocusing. As a result, dancers who train in a "task-involving climate" experience more enjoyment, less stress, higher levels of self-esteem and better body images.
- **Ego-Involving Climate:** On the other hand, an "ego-involving climate" is created by teachers who encourage rivalry among dancers, punish mistakes, value the contributions of the most talented dancers and place great emphasis and reward on outcomes. Dancers who train in these types of environments experience more stress, less enjoyment, lower levels of self-esteem and more body dissatisfaction.

STANDARDS, FEEDBACK, AUTHORITY AND VALUES

The interaction of environment (climate) and personality has a powerful impact upon performance. While teachers may not be able to change the personality of dancers, they are in a position to use their standards, feedback, authority and values to create a task-involving climate.

CREATING AND MAINTAINING STUDIO STANDARDS

When defining and communicating a teaching philosophy, it is important to create fair and impartial standards. In order to accomplish this, teachers must first define their personal set of values, morals and ethical codes. For instance, is teaching life skills through dance important to you or do you prefer to focus solely on performance outcomes? If students break the rules or have poor behavior in the studio, how will you respond? Do you believe that all dancers should have an opportunity to perform or should there be a competitive process? Teachers need to be clear about how the large issues will be handled and develop consistent disciplinary procedures. This clarity will help insure that situations are being responded to in an ethical and non-emotional manner.

Teachers need to clearly communicate their teaching philosophy to both students and parents. To this end, parent conferences are helpful, as are brochures and handbooks. Dancer handbooks can contain information on: a) roles of dancers and parents, b) expectations for behavior, c) expectations for practice and performance, d) disciplinary procedures, e) chain of command for complaints, f) standards for selection of parts and g) preferred way to be contacted.

PROVIDING CONSTRUCTIVE FEEDBACK

When providing feedback, start with a genuine positive and avoid negative attacks. One strategy is to provide feedback in the form of three pluses and a wish (Positive Coaching Alliance). For example, "You have improved your turnout, given 100 percent effort during practice and are very supportive of the other dancers. In the future, I wish that you would be kinder to yourself when you make mistakes." Provide feedback to parents and dancers in a forthright and non-emotional manner and be sure to temper responses to mistakes.

Often, parents and dancers need assistance in redefining how they measure "success." Sometimes success can be measured by assignment of parts or skill progression. At other times, effort, openness to learning and ability to perform under pressure must be valued. By balancing attention on outcomes with acknowledgement of performance improvements and mental strengths, teachers help dancers and parents maintain perspective.

RECOGNIZING AND DIRECTING AUTHORITY

Discipline can only be effective when a connection between teacher and student is present. Therefore, teachers need to recognize and seek opportunities to connect emotionally with their dancers. They can do so by acknowledging students' thoughts and opinions and validating their feelings, even the imperfect ones (i.e. anger, frustration, fear, doubt and isolation). Encourage a collaborative relationship among teacher, dancer and parents by reminding all parties of their shared goals. At times, there may be conflicts about how to meet these goals, but conflict negotiated effectively can deepen and strengthen relationships. Teachers should respond to dancers and parents rationally rather than emotionally and provide dancers with direction on how to strengthen their attitudes by modeling optimism. The ways in which a teacher manages frustration, deals with pressure, responds to negative events and refocuses are constantly on display.

Teachers have numerous responsibilities as they attempt to meet dancers' physical and emotional needs. Teachers should be sure to connect with local resources so that they can maintain their focus on what they do best—teaching. They should develop a list of local psychologists, nutritionists, sports medicine specialists, physical therapists, acupuncturists and exercise physiologists, among others, to whom they refer dancers.

HELPING STUDENTS RECOGNIZE AND DEFINE THEIR VALUES

Teachers have an opportunity to help young people define their values and behave in accordance with those beliefs. When students' actions match their values, they are living their lives with integrity. Teachers can show dancers that they value them as people by recognizing all aspects of their personality. While dance is a large part of their lives, they are also children, sisters, brothers, students, volunteers in the community, athletes and friends.

QUICK TIPS FOR TEACHERS

- **Be a good role model.** There is a saying, "Smile. Your dancers are watching you." Children learn various ways to deal with strong emotions by watching how their teachers react to difficult situations. When dealing with a student who is particularly hard to handle, for example, teachers should take a deep breath, use a refocus point or take a personal time-out.
- **Acknowledge mistakes as part of learning.** Teachers should use success *and* failure in a productive manner. After both good and poor performances, teachers can identify controllable aspects of the performance, give corrections and create future performance goals.
- **Set effective goals.** Most dancers set *outcome goals* (for example, "I want to be the principal dancer."). In addition, dancers must be taught to set *performance goals* (for example, "In order to be chosen as principal, I need to work on my flexibility.") and *task goals* ("Today, I will stretch for an extra 20 minutes, breathe when frustrated and use positive self-talk during rehearsal.").
- **Focus on corrections.** Find opportunities to praise good behavior and point out progress. Assist dancers by giving specific corrections and validate forward movement. This reminds dancers that improvement is a process.

DEVELOPING GOOD RELATIONSHIPS WITH PARENTS

Communication between parents and teachers is of critical importance. A dancer's performance is affected not only by his/her personality, but also by the environment in which s/he trains. When a mutual understanding exists between teacher and parent, the student's dance experience can be enhanced on many levels.

Parents and dance instructors can and should work together in a productive manner to effectively meet the needs of the young dancer. In order to do this, each party must consider the different agendas and preconceived notions they bring to the table. Parents can feel anxious about talking with instructors because they may feel responsible if their child is unable to meet expectations or has a poor attitude. In essence, they may worry that others perceive them to be deficient in the parenting department. Many times parents leave teacher conferences bewildered by the teacher's criticisms of their child and torn between conflicting views held by their child and the teacher.

Teachers, on the other hand, may have questions directed at them by dissatisfied parents. This can leave them feeling criticized and undervalued. They may view certain questions on the part of parents to be attacks on their decision-making or teaching tactics.

Parents and teachers do share some common interests. It's helpful for teachers to express concerns early before a crisis occurs. The same holds true for parents, as they should inform teachers of potential pitfalls—both emotional and physical. Parents possess important information about their child, as do teachers. Exchanges of information without blaming and finger-pointing can lead to productive problem solving.

It's important for parents to leave a conference with understanding and balanced feedback. Teachers can share with parents the concepts being taught in rehearsal (i.e., focus, managing frustration, paying attention to the positive, etc.) and ask for parents to reinforce these concepts at home.

FIVE STEPS TO USE IN PARENT-TEACHER CONFERENCES

1. Start with what is going well. (For example, "Shelley is a joy to have in the class. She has a strong work ethic and is open to learning.")
2. Show concern. (For example, "I'm concerned about a specific pattern of behavior and hoping you can provide some insight.")
3. Express concerns about behaviors. (For example, "When Shelley makes a mistake, she cries inconsolably. The other day it became extreme when she fell to the floor and curled up in the fetal position.")
4. Validate what the parents are saying. (For example, "So, what I hear you saying is that you have seen this behavior before but it's quite infrequent.")
5. Brainstorm next steps.

PRINT IT! A WORKSHEET FOR PARENTS

ENCOURAGING EXCELLENCE WITHOUT BECOMING A STAGE PARENT—**A.F.F.I.R.M.**

Give Affection regardless of performance outcome. Children need to know that their failures and successes don't affect parental support, love or acceptance. Unconditional parental love gives kids a safe haven from which to launch lofty dreams and ambitions. Conversely, children who believe that mom or dad values them more with every ribbon and trophy will most likely buckle under the weight of unrealistic expectations. Express unconditional love by communicating to your children that your love is based on who they are rather than what they accomplish. The pursuit of excellence is then transformed from a daunting task to a realistic goal.

Be Focused, but don't coach. It is the parents' job to develop the child and the coach's job to develop the dancer. Stay away from detailed, technical discussions about performance. Instead, encourage your child to establish good and realistic goal-setting habits.

Be Flexible. At the first sign of success, single-minded parents place their budding dancers on the fast track without taking time to find out the child's goals and objectives—and without discussing the time frame with the teacher! Allow your agenda to be set by what is best for your child's long-term health and well being, not by short-term goals. Being flexible enables both you and your child to enjoy the journey more fully.

Interact without dominating the conversation. A supportive parent listens more and talks less. Parents provide great comfort for children by creating a safe environment in which children know it is acceptable to express true feelings of loss and disappointment. A key element in establishing that safe environment is learning to listen. Listen for descriptive words that express how your children feel about themselves and their performances. By listening, you communicate that their thoughts and feelings are worthy of expression and you respect their experience.

Reframe. It's the parents' role to provide perspective. Remind your children of the bigger picture, which includes long-term goals and other aspects of their life such as academics, friendships, family, health and spirituality. Your guidance and feedback affirms that dance is only one aspect of a multidimensional life. This truth serves as a valuable balance to the pressures of competition.

Model. Parents are some of the most powerful role models for children. Kids learn valuable coping skills watching mom and dad deal with difficult situations. Live your own life with integrity by insuring that your actions correspond with your values and beliefs. When you make mistakes, admit your errors, and explain to your child the more appropriate response. Your personal life experiences can provide powerful learning opportunities for your children.

CHILDREN WITH SPECIAL LEARNING NEEDS

Children differ in their capabilities to sustain attention, control impulses, manage distractions, sort relevant information and comprehend and follow rules. When trying to teach to a wide variety of attention styles, teachers can help students by identifying individual strengths and special learning needs, and by designing teaching plans to mobilize individual strengths.

When teaching children with special learning needs—like Attention Deficit Disorder (ADD) or Asperger's Syndrome—be sure to keep the class structured and organized. Rules and expectations need to be clearly communicated. Tasks can be made manageable by breaking them into smaller, less complex demands. Reinforcement for completed tasks is critical. Starting each class or activity with something they can successfully accomplish can assist children who lack confidence.

Cooperative learning can be an effective way to increase attention and allows dancers to share their strengths with one another. Help students transition from one part of rehearsal to another by warning them a few minutes prior to changing activities. Students will benefit from variety in teaching methods. Teachers can verbally explain a movement, show the movement and have the students walk through the movement, watch it, picture it and even draw it.

Teachers can help students with ADD or other special learning needs by periodically reminding them of the task/correction; calling them by name and then pausing before giving more information; placing them in close proximity to you in the studio; maintaining eye contact; and using gestures. Recent research suggests that providing more stimulation and variety can improve the performance and behavior of students with ADD.

CHAPTER 12: Nutrition

INTRODUCTION

In general, a dancer's diet should be composed of about 55-60 percent carbohydrates, 12-15 percent protein and 20-30 percent fat, with adequate fluid intake. A well-balanced diet is vital to a dancer. Carbohydrates and fat provide the energy needed to perform exercises in class and during rehearsals. Protein is required to provide the structural building blocks of the cells and also to work as enzymes to help break down carbohydrates and fat to produce energy. There are micronutrients in food that are important to the health of bones, nerves and muscles. Adequate amounts of these micronutrients are needed to ensure optimal performance. Because all functions in the body take place in an aqueous (water) environment, adequate fluid intake is essential to maintain the body's hydration to ensure the ability to perform at one's best.

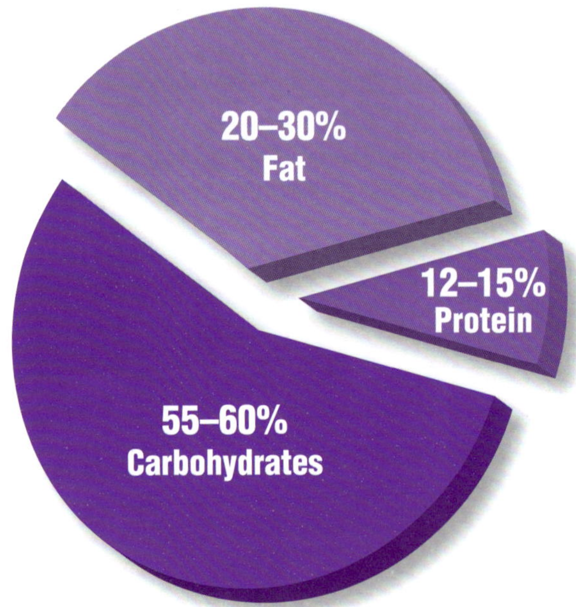

CARBOHYDRATES

WHAT ARE CARBOHYDRATES AND WHY ARE THEY VITAL FOR BODY FUNCTION?

- Carbohydrates in the diet are sugars, starches and fiber. After digestion, sugars and starches are stored in muscles. The breakdown of carbohydrates provides the primary fuel for muscles to contract and move the body.
- Examples of carbohydrates: Breads, pasta, rice, fruits and vegetables. Whole grains and fresh fruits and vegetables are rich sources of fiber, which helps food move through the digestive tract.
- Food choices should be nutrient-dense carbohydrates (whole-grain bread/pasta, fruits and vegetables), because they contain vitamins and minerals. Simple sugars (candy, table sugar and soda) are also carbohydrates, but they are nutrient-poor.

HOW MUCH DO YOU NEED AND WHY?

- Dancers should get 55-60 percent of their daily calories from carbohydrates, with the lower end of the range during regular training and the high end during intense training.
- Insufficient carbohydrate intake leads to fatigue during classes and rehearsals, because carbohydrates provide the fuel for exercise.
- A carbohydrate snack before class, such as an energy bar, can provide energy boosts for class and rehearsal. During class, simple sugars may provide an energy boost. Carbohydrates in a liquid solution provide the added benefit of fluid replacement.
- A high-carbohydrate diet improves performance and enhances ability to train, because carbohydrates provide energy to muscle.
- Although carbohydrates are an important energy source for muscles, without sufficient fat and protein in the diet, carbohydrates will not be as effective. This is because protein is needed for muscle structure and also to make enzymes that are involved in metabolism. Fats are also an energy source and are needed for other important processes in the body, as will be described below.

FATS

WHAT ARE FATS AND WHY ARE THEY VITAL FOR BODY FUNCTION?

Fat is a component of all cells. It is needed for hormone production and absorption of fat-soluble vitamins, and is an important fuel for muscles—especially during long rehearsals. The muscles can store and break down fat to provide energy for muscle contraction and movement.

HOW MUCH DO YOU NEED AND WHY?

- About 20-30 percent of the diet should be fat.
- Unsaturated fats are the healthiest fats and are found mainly in fish, nuts, seeds and oils from plants. There are two types of unsaturated fats: monounsaturated fats, which include olive oil, canola oil, nuts, seeds (e.g., sesame) and avocado, and polyunsaturated fats, which include safflower oil, sunflower oil, corn oil, polyunsaturated margarine, walnuts, sunflower seeds and oily fish such as sardines and salmon. Fats that should be limited in the diet are saturated fats, which are found in animal sources (butter fat, beef fat, chicken fat).
- A diet too low in fat can have serious health consequences and ultimately can impair performance.

PROTEINS

WHAT ARE PROTEINS AND WHY ARE THEY VITAL FOR BODY FUNCTION?

Proteins provide structural components of cells and are important for muscle contraction. Proteins are used to make the enzymes that are needed for metabolism.

- For non-vegetarians, chicken and turkey (without the skin) are excellent low-fat protein sources.
- For vegetarians, tofu, seitan (wheat gluten) and mixtures of beans and rice are good protein choices.

HOW MUCH DO YOU NEED AND WHY?

- About 12-15 percent of the diet should be protein.
- Protein is needed to repair stressed muscles and to make enzymes necessary for metabolism. These enzymes are needed for muscles to break down fat and carbohydrates.
- Protein powders are not necessary for male dancers at any age, if they are following the recommendations for dietary protein. Some adolescent boys believe they need more protein to build muscle mass, but if they are getting sufficient protein in their diet, they do not need protein supplements. Girls do not generally believe they need protein and, hence, may not be getting sufficient protein in their diet. If a protein supplement is warranted, the best choice is milk powder.

VITAMINS AND MINERALS

WHAT ARE VITAMINS AND MINERALS AND WHY ARE THEY VITAL FOR BODY FUNCTION?

Vitamins and minerals are micronutrients that are essential to one's health and are needed by the body in small quantities. They are present in food, and food—not supplements—is the best way to get vitamins and minerals.

HOW MUCH DO YOU NEED AND WHY?

The amount of micronutrients needed differs for each vitamin and mineral. Amounts also differ over age. Eat a diet rich in a wide variety of vegetables, fruits, dairy products and whole grains to get enough vitamins and minerals. A daily multivitamin and mineral supplement is okay to use as an "insurance policy."

- The B vitamins play important roles in energy production (especially thiamin, riboflavin, niacin and Vitamin B6) and in red blood cell formation (Vitamin B12 plus folic acid).
- Vitamins A (beta carotene), C and E are necessary for the repair of over-stressed muscles and are needed to help muscles recover from strenuous classes and rehearsals. Vitamin D is important in bone formation.

- Calcium, iron and zinc are a few of the many minerals that are important for dancers' health and performance. Calcium is important for building strong bones. Iron is important for red blood cells, because iron is a component of hemoglobin in red blood cells. Zinc helps the muscles produce energy by assisting several enzymes in metabolism. Many dancers do not get enough calcium, iron and zinc.
- The richest source of calcium is dairy products. Red meat is a rich source of iron and zinc, but vegetarians can ingest whole grains in whole-grain bread to get these minerals.
- Deficiency of vitamins and minerals can impair performance. If dancers believe that they are deficient in a certain vitamin/mineral, they could take a multivitamin/mineral that contains less than 100 percent of the recommended level (RDA or Recommended Daily Allowance) of any vitamin or mineral (the percent of each vitamin and mineral is specified on the label). Dancers should not take individual vitamins or minerals (for example, just riboflavin or zinc) because this could disrupt the natural balance in their bodies. The vitamins and minerals found in healthy foods are best for the body. If a dancer thinks s/he has a vitamin deficiency, it is best to consult a nutritionist before taking large doses of a supplement.

FLUIDS

WHAT ARE FLUIDS AND WHY ARE THEY VITAL FOR BODY FUNCTION?

Fluids are liquids that are consumed, like water, fruit juice, milk and sports drinks. They keep the body, which is about two-thirds water, hydrated and functioning. Dehydration is a condition that occurs when a person loses more fluid than s/he takes in. When the body becomes dehydrated, performance in class and onstage can deteriorate.

HOW MUCH DO YOU NEED AND WHY?

- Under conditions of only mild exercise and sweat loss, men should consume about 13 cups of total beverages a day and women should consume about nine cups of total beverages a day.
- Sweat is the primary means the body has to cool itself during exercise. Because sweat losses can be substantial during a hard class or long rehearsal, it is important to drink fluids to meet this loss. Dancers should check their urine color to determine if they are dehydrated. A clear or pale yellow indicates adequate hydration. Dark yellow suggests dehydration.
- Fluid loss results in dehydration that can impair performance and mental functioning, such as the ability to quickly pick up complicated class combinations and choreography, and execute them effectively.
- Small amounts (about 1⁄2 cup) of fluid should be consumed every 15 minutes during rigorous exercise and sweating. A water bottle or sports drink should be part of a dancer's "gear," and, if possible, the dancer should be able to bring the bottle into the studio for frequent drinks.
- Following class and rehearsal, dancers should continue to increase fluid consumption for the next few hours. Avoid carbonated drinks and large quantities of fruit juice that are high in calories and could cause diarrhea (some fruit juice is fine, as juices can be rich in Vitamin C). Instead, drink water and sports drinks. Sports drinks provide the body with electrolytes (salts) important for rehydration and have only modest amounts of sugar.

DIETARY SUPPLEMENTS

WHAT ARE DIETARY SUPPLEMENTS AND WHY ARE THEY NOT VITAL FOR BODY FUNCTION?

- Dietary supplements range from vitamin and mineral supplements to supplements containing dietary ingredients marketed as a way to enhance performance (build muscle, increase energy or improve recovery) or decrease body weight.
- Most supplements have never been proven to fulfill these claims. Many of these supplements are ineffective; some are even dangerous. Dietary supplements can be legally marketed without adequate proof that they are effective or safe, and they may contain contaminants not listed on the label.
- Only the supplement creatine has sufficient evidence to support that it can increase strength or benefit the types of high bursts of energy activity that dancers perform. However, creatine is associated with an increase in body weight that may be due to increased water retention by the muscles. Natural sources of creatine include meat, fish and poultry.

CALORIC REQUIREMENTS PER DAY

BOYS AND GIRLS

- Boys and girls 4-6 years old need about 46 calories per pound of body weight.
  Boys and girls 7-10 years old need about 32 calories per pound of body weight.
- The carbohydrate, fat and protein needs are the same for boys and girls.
- Adolescents, especially girls, should eat foods high in calcium (milk, yogurt, dairy products) that insure bone building.

PRE-PROFESSIONAL AND RECREATIONAL

- Young active adult women and teens need about 17 calories per pound of body weight.
  Young active adult men and teens need about 18 calories per pound of body weight.

PRE-PROFESSIONAL TO PROFESSIONAL

- A female dancer during heavy training needs about 22 calories per pound of body weight.
  A male dancer during heavy training needs about 24 calories per pound of body weight.

TIPS FOR TALKING TO DANCERS AND PARENTS ABOUT NUTRITION:

- Stress the importance of ingesting sufficient calories and plenty of fruits, vegetables, protein, dairy products and whole grains to meet the demands of exercise so dancers can perform at their best.
- If a teacher suspects a problem with weight control (a dancer is too thin or too heavy), s/he should refer the dancer to a qualified nutritionist and/or to his/her physician.

CHAPTER 13: Principles of Training

INTRODUCTION

The major objective in any kind of training, whether it is ballet, basketball or tennis, is to enable the body to adapt to improve the performance of specific tasks required by the activity. Ballet training must encompass many components to adequately prepare the dancer's body for the varied tasks that ballet requires. Outside of the typical ballet class, the dance student can cross-train by participating in other physical activities to help the body adapt to ballet more effectively and with fewer injuries. Cross-training can include cardiovascular endurance activities, strength training and flexibility training. However, first it is important to understand some basic conditioning principles that can be applied to ballet class as well as to cross-training activities.

FIVE BASIC CONDITIONING PRINCIPLES

1. Always Warm Up

A warm-up eases the body into exercise by gradually increasing heart rate and circulation. It prepares the systems of the body slowly rather than taxing them suddenly. The best way for the dancer to warm up is to work the large muscle groups continuously for 15 minutes. This increases circulation and blood flow to the muscles, making the muscles more pliable. It is good to stretch after the warm-up period. (*Note:* The body cannot become properly warmed up with heating pads and/or clothing only.)

Students should be encouraged to warm up before class. However, the teacher should still organize class so that his/her students' bodies are gradually warmed up before s/he begins asking for more difficult positions, extreme stretches or complex coordination. Students also must be aware that it is their responsibility to warm up again before rehearsals. The body will cool down in 30 minutes, so if the dancer has a 30-minute break, s/he will need to warm up and stretch again. The teacher should take this into consideration when scheduling classes and rehearsals.

Sample Warm-up Exercise: A simple way to warm up is to prance around the room while gently swinging your arms.

2. Progress Slowly (Gradualness)

It takes six to eight weeks for a dancer to get into top condition, so progress students slowly when they are coming back from vacation or injury. Add small daily increments of exercise to ramp up to a full schedule of daily class plus rehearsal, if appropriate.

3. Watch Out For Fatigue

A tired dancer is more prone to injury. A long rehearsal day or a day filled with classes may be too much for a dancer who is not used to the intensity those schedules require. (See "Progress Slowly.")

4. Cool Down

Gradually diminishing the intensity of work allows the body to slow down all of its systems, including circulation. A good way to cool down is to actively stretch the body.

5. Recondition

It only takes one to two weeks to lose some of your fitness. This does not mean that a dancer should not take time off; it simply means that activities have to be ramped up appropriately when returning to dance training. There must be a reconditioning time period.

TRAINING GUIDELINES (FOR DANCE CLASSES AND CONDITIONING)

When increasing the difficulty of a dancer's ballet class or adding more classes into his/her daily or weekly practice, follow these two guidelines so that the dancer has a reduced chance of injury and can benefit completely from the added workout.

Note: An excessive volume of training, or a rapid increase in the rate of training, may contribute to the onset of overuse injuries. There is a consensus among those in the sports medicine field that young athletes or dancers training more than 20 hours per week should be monitored closely for increased risk of overuse injuries and other factors such as delayed onset of menarche (a girl's first menstrual period).

1. Increase only one of the following components at a time:

- Intensity: Difficulty of class
- Duration: Length of class
- Frequency: Number of classes

Example: If a dancer is used to taking two classes a week, it is not advisable to suddenly increase frequency to daily classes. Instead, slowly add classes over a two- to three-week period to allow the dancer's body to adjust. If a teacher suddenly increases frequency to daily classes, then s/he should decrease the intensity and/or duration of each class while the dancer's body adjusts to the new schedule.

In general, the volume or intensity of training should not increase more than 10 percent per week. A student who is expected to attend a summer training program where s/he will be training 20-28 hours per week (much more than the usual average of 12-14 hours per week), should also gradually progress the number of hours s/he trains over the weeks or months prior to the summer session.

2. Specificity of Training

The dancer's body must have time to adapt to new choreography or technique so it does not become injured. The dance teacher can help by altering the content of class to incorporate a specific task or technique before the dancer begins rehearsing that task or technique.

Cross-Training

INTRODUCTION

Dance students can benefit from building strength, flexibility and cardiovascular endurance inside and outside of the ballet studio. The following three types of training—cardiovascular, strength and flexibility—can help improve overall fitness, prevent injuries and improve dancing in general.

CARDIOVASCULAR ENDURANCE

WHAT IS CARDIOVASCULAR ENDURANCE?

When you train to increase cardiovascular endurance, you are improving the ability of the heart, circulatory system and respiratory system to supply oxygen and fuel to the muscles at a steady rate for a considerable length of time. Cardiovascular training increases your ability to dance for longer periods of time without getting fatigued, which decreases the possibility of getting injured.

CARDIOVASCULAR ENDURANCE IMPROVES...

- ...efficiency of the lungs in supplying oxygen to the blood.
- ...ability of the heart to pump more blood.
- ...ability of the blood vessels to carry more blood.
- ...efficiency of the circulatory system, which delivers blood to the muscles and then returns it to the heart.
- ...ability of the muscles to extract oxygen from the blood.

WHAT CAN DANCERS DO TO BUILD CARDIOVASCULAR ENDURANCE?

Dancers often do not have the chance to develop cardiovascular endurance in ballet class. Ballet class is composed of short bursts of intense activity lasting only a few minutes, and it takes at least 15 minutes of steady activity to reach the point at which you are building endurance. In other words, ballet class is more anaerobic than aerobic. Since dancers often get injured when they are fatigued, it is important to supplement ballet training with aerobic activities. Cross-training for cardiovascular fitness will help improve endurance and decrease fatigue while rehearsing and performing.

Note: Aerobic metabolism is dependent upon oxygen and involves the ability of the muscles to use oxygen in the process of generating energy for endurance activities. By contrast, anaerobic metabolism requires no oxygen to generate energy within the muscles, but it is less efficient and can only be used for short periods before the muscles run out of that source of energy. Anaerobic metabolism is essential for activities of high intensity and short duration.

Students should be encouraged to bike, swim or use aerobic equipment (for example: treadmills, elliptical devices and bikes) at a gym for 30 minutes, three to five times a week. As with all new activities, the dancer should start this program slowly with ten minutes of an activity every other day, and not at the same time that s/he is performing or beginning a new course of dance training.

The very young dancer (5 to 11 or 12 years old) does not need to engage in formal aerobic training but should be encouraged to be active outside of ballet. This will aid in well-balanced development of motor coordination and perhaps help in avoiding burnout from early intense specialization.

STRENGTH TRAINING

WHAT IS STRENGTH TRAINING?

Gaining muscle strength will help a dancer move more efficiently and will help protect his/her bones and joints, too. It is important to realize that the proper strengthening of a muscle will not reduce movement speed or flexibility. A muscle can be both strong and flexible, but both components must be properly trained. Finding a balance between strength and flexibility will help a dancer avoid injury. Below we have provided some guidelines for strength training specific to a dancer's age and gender.

Note: Finding trained professionals within your community, including athletic trainers, physical therapists, clinical exercise physiologists and various other well-trained and credentialed exercise instructors, can be a valuable resource. Also, refer to the addendum (page 92) for strength-training guidelines for young athletes from the National Strength and Conditioning Association (NSCA).

WHAT CAN DANCERS DO TO BUILD STRENGTH?

Specific strength training is not necessary during the early years of dance (5 to 11 or 12 years old). However, beginning at age 11 or 12 it can be beneficial to add strength training outside of dance class to improve overall health and fitness for recreational dancers, and to help prepare pre-professional dancers for a professional career with fewer injuries.

PHOTO 14. Push-ups with knees on floor

A good way to begin strength training is to use the dancer's own body weight rather than using free weights or resistance machines. For example, doing push-ups with knees on the floor is an excellent way for dancers to gain arm strength while stabilizing the trunk, which is also beneficial. [See PHOTO 14.] As with all exercise programs, the dancer should be cautioned to progress very slowly. Add small daily increments of work and remember that it takes six to eight weeks to get into top condition.

SPECIFIC AREAS THAT NEED STRENGTHENING IN DANCERS OVER 11 OR 12

All dancers, male and female, over the age of 11 or 12, can benefit from strength training in the following areas of the body:

- **Ankles and feet:** It is imperative that male and female dancers have strong ankles and feet, as they are the areas of the body that most often get injured in dancers. Ballet demands very flexible feet and ankles, which can make them more susceptible to injury unless they are very strong. One way to achieve this is to do Theraband ankle exercises:

1. Pointing: Put the Theraband around your toes with your leg stretched out in front of you.

Step 1: Point your ankle and foot, leaving your toes flexed. [See PHOTO 15.]

Step 2: Point your toes. [See PHOTO 16.]

Step 3: Flex only your toes up. (This is the same position as in step 1.)

Step 4: Flex your foot from your ankle. [See PHOTO 17.]

Start the cycle again. Each step should be slow and controlled.

2. Winging: Tie a piece of Theraband in a loop and place it around both of your feet.

With your ankles, feet and toes pointed, wing one foot out to the side and slowly return to neutral. Repeat with the other foot. [See PHOTO 18.]

You can also do this exercise with your feet not fully pointed—in different degrees of flexion—but you absolutely must include the fully-pointed position.

PHOTO 15. Pointing step 1

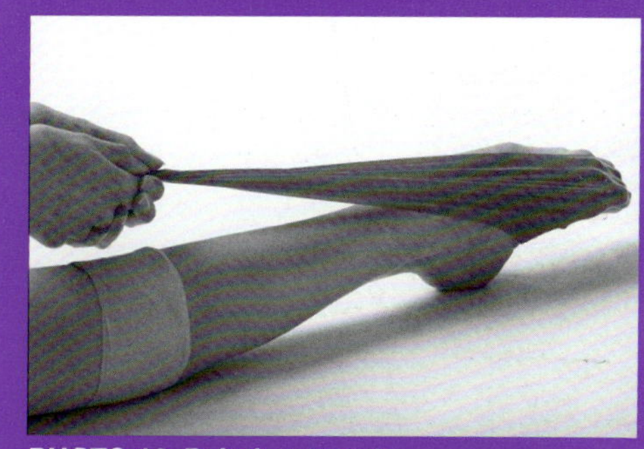
PHOTO 16. Pointing step 2

PHOTO 17. Pointing step 4

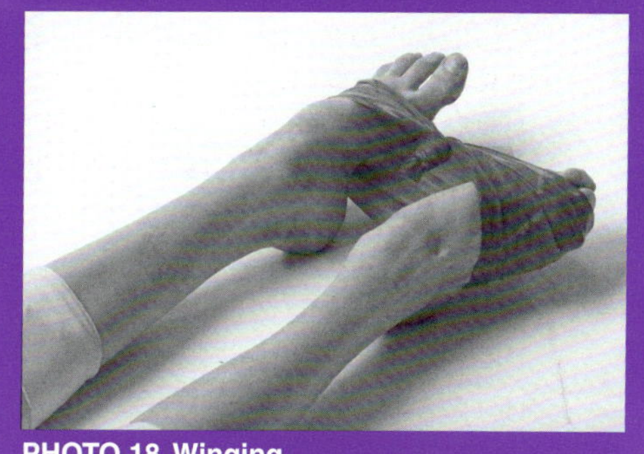
PHOTO 18. Winging

- **Core (abdominals, back and pelvis):** Strong core muscles—including your abdominals, back, pelvic floor and hips—provide support to the spine for everything from walking, lifting and standing to sitting upright. Weak core muscles may lead to poor posture, lower-back pain and injury. Dancers—especially young dancers—typically have weak abdominals. An indication that a dancer is having trouble stabilizing the core is when s/he is having difficulty maintaining pelvic position from plié to relevé and in landing from jumps.

  There are currently many core-strengthening programs (for example, Pilates and Gyrotonics) that can be helpful to dancers. These exercise systems can be very valuable if the instructor is well-trained and the exercise level is appropriate for the individual. Private lessons are often better because group classes don't always take into consideration the level of the students, and therefore may lead to injury. It is probably not appropriate for very young dancers to attempt these methods because they require difficult coordination and attention to detail.

Side Bridge

1. Start on your right side, propped up on the right elbow with the left hand holding the right shoulder.

2. Place the left foot on the floor slightly in front of the right, in parallel.

3. Lift your hips off the floor to create a straight line from the tip of the head to the feet. [See PHOTO 19.]

4. Hold for 5-10 seconds; repeat 10 times.

5. Do not let your body rotate at your torso.

6. If this position is too difficult to maintain, start with your knees bent and lift hips off the floor so that you create a straight line from the tip of your head to your knees.

PHOTO 19. Side Bridge

Bridge

1. Start on your back with knees bent. Feet should be flat on the floor and hip distance apart. Arms should be resting at your sides.

2. Pull in your abdominals, then lift your pelvis off the floor to create a straight line from your neck to your knees. [See PHOTO 20.]

3. Don't over-arch your back.

4. Hold 5-10 seconds and then slowly lower down.

PHOTO 20. Bridge

You can make this exercise more challenging by lifting one leg at a time off the floor, after you're in the bridge position. Make sure that you are keeping your pelvis level as you lift each leg. Do not let the pelvis rotate. You can monitor this by putting your fingers on each side of your pelvic bone.

Plank

1. Start in a push-up position.

2. Maintain the normal curves of your spine. Do not sway the back or let the shoulder blades wing (protrude). [See PHOTO 21.]

3. Hold the plank position for 5-10 seconds. Repeat 10 times or as many times as you can while maintaining the proper alignment. Put knees on floor when you need to rest.

4. If the exercise is too difficult to do while maintaining the proper alignment, start in a modified push-up position (with knees on floor). [See PHOTO 22.]

PHOTO 21. Plank

PHOTO 22. Modified Plank

Curl-up

1. Start on your back with knees bent and feet flat on the floor, hip-width apart. Hands are behind your head.

2. Initiate the curl-up on the exhale by pulling in your deep abdominals (drawing your belly button toward your spine). Let your top front ribs relax into your chest and curl up until your shoulder blades are off the floor. [See PHOTO 23.] The movement should create a smooth, even curve from the base of the spine through the top of your head. Your stomach should not be bulging up; it should be pulled toward the floor.

3. Try to bring your trunk up without tucking your pelvis under. Your pelvis should remain in a neutral position.

4. Breathe in as you return to the floor, attempting to keep the abdominals engaged.

PHOTO 23. Curl-up

5. You can try to vary the breathing, which will make the exercise more challenging. You can also hold at the top while you inhale and exhale, and then return to the start position.

6. Repeat the same steps but add rotation. Bring your left ribcage toward the right side of your pelvis and vice versa.

- **Hyper-mobility:** Excellent flexibility is desirable in a dancer. But hypermobile individuals are at increased risk for joint injuries because of the possibility for extremes of motion. These dancers should be encouraged to strength train outside of dance class.

STRENGTH TRAINING: GENDER-SPECIFIC ISSUES

In ballet, boys and girls have different work loads that require specific attention in strengthening. For example, boys are required to lift the girls in partnering and girls have to dance en pointe.

BOYS

- **Core strength:** This is vital to protect the back during partnering. If a boy cannot maintain his trunk position in normal ballet class, he will not be able to support his trunk in partnering.
- **Shoulder strength**: Ballet class does not typically incorporate much upper-body strengthening, which is essential for partnering. The male dancer needs to do additional upper-body strengthening to help protect the shoulders.

GIRLS

- **Core strength:** Female dancers in their preteens and teens have a higher risk of stress fractures in the low back than the normal population because of the increased forces placed on the low back when dancing. Core strengthening and correct placement can diminish the likelihood of back injuries. (Note: This can also occur in boys.)
- **Bone density:** Slender females with abnormal menstrual cycles (see "Menstrual Cycle" and "Female Athlete Triad") are at increased risk for osteopenia and osteoporosis. Young dancers in their teens can benefit from lifting light weights, which helps build bone density.
- **Lean body mass:** The human body is composed of fat and lean body mass. Lean body mass refers to the sum of everything other than fat—an individual's bones, muscles and organs. Lean body mass can be increased through strength training. Exercise physiologists have shown that strength training in conjunction with a cardiovascular workout is an excellent way to control weight. However, if a girl is already underweight and you have concerns about her eating behavior, be mindful that adding additional physical activity can be a problem. And as always, any concerns about eating behavior and weight should be brought up with the appropriate health-care professional.
- **Shoulder stabilization:** Female ballet dancers do not typically need great arm strength. However, since female dancers often have joints that are hyper-lax (overly-flexible), they may benefit from some basic shoulder stabilization exercises. These exercises will prevent shoulder injuries that can happen while partnering or while dancing choreography with atypical or fast arm movements.

PARTNERING ISSUES

- Boys are often behind in technical training because of starting later.
- Boys may begin partnering before their growth spurt. This means they don't have the strength gains that occur after the growth spurt to help them manage partnering.
- Boys are often behind in physical development compared to girls.
- Young girls are often inexperienced in partnering.

SOLUTIONS TO PARTNERING ISSUES

- Encourage or develop a strength-training program for boys.
- If possible, begin training girls with more experienced partners.
- Appropriately pair dancers for size, weight and strength development, not by age.
- Limit partnering to shift-of-weight exercises, simple lifts and other activities that don't require great strength if a dancer does not have the requisite strength.

STRENGTH-TRAINING PRECAUTIONS

As with every type of exercise, there is a risk of injury when training. The following precautions for strength training have been specifically written for dancers:

- Use lower loads to protect hyper-lax (overly-flexible) joints.
- Be aware of the prevalence of long lever arms (dancers tend to have very long limbs, which take more strength to control). Be careful not to add too much weight, especially during growth spurts. Repeated developpés without proper trunk control can cause hip tendonitis. The dancer must slowly build the strength to hold the leg in full extension.
- Use small increments when progressing, such as a five to ten percent increase in weight.
- Don't increase weights, repetitions and sets at the same time.
- Focus on trunk control (abdominal and pelvic muscles). Target the core muscles with Pilates, Gyrotonics or physioball exercises and make sure the dancer is performing all exercises with correct posture. (No swayback.)
- During the growth spurt, be more cautious. Focus on motor control versus strength training.

ADDENDUM

Strength-training guidelines adapted from the National Strength and Conditioning Association (NSCA).

- The dancer should be adequately mature, both physiologically and psychologically, to comply with coaching instructions.
- A pre-participation exam by the dancer's physician, likely done as part of the dance school's protocol, should address the issue of strength training.
- Qualified instructors are essential. Ask to see the credentials and/or certification documents of the instructors.
- The goals and expectations of a strength-training program for a dancer should be clearly understood.
- A comprehensive fitness program including cardiovascular workout should be delineated.
- A five- to ten-minute warm-up should precede the strength-training activities.
- Strength training should be done two to three days a week non-consecutively.
- Vary the muscle groups being strengthened: for example, upper body, lower body and core.
- To assure maximum benefit with the least risk, make sure proper form and technique are used with light loads (weights).

- Sets should be gradually increased from six to 15 repetitions per set. A set equals a group of repetitions performed continuously without stopping.
- There should be appropriate periodization throughout the year. Periodization is the process of varying a training program at regular time intervals to bring about optimal gains in physical performance.

FLEXIBILITY TRAINING

WHAT IS FLEXIBILITY TRAINING?

Flexibility is defined as the range of movement of a specific joint or joints influenced by the associated bones, muscles, tendons and ligaments surrounding those joints. The greatest gains in flexibility can be achieved by stretching muscle. Tendons will stretch only minimally and ligaments even less. Because ligaments provide much of the stability of a joint, it is not safe to overstretch them. Overstretching ligaments can lead to joint damage. For example, once a dancer sprains an ankle, that ankle is more susceptible to repeated sprains. The sprain overstretches the ligaments (in this case in a traumatic way) or worse, tears the ligament so the ankle joint no longer has the stability it previously had.

WHAT CAN DANCERS DO TO INCREASE FLEXIBILITY?

There is currently some controversy in the sports medicine literature that is raising questions about the best way to stretch and how much stretching is helpful versus harmful.

As of now, there are no definitive answers. However, since ballet requires extreme joint positions, stretching is a requirement. Below, we provide some general guidelines to keep students from getting hurt while increasing flexibility. It is important to recognize that some individuals are already extremely flexible. These individuals should use stretching only as part of a prudent warm-up. Attempts to increase flexibility in the hypermobile individual can be a recipe for disaster.

THREE TYPES OF STRETCHING

Greater gains in flexibility of a muscle can be achieved when the muscle is warm. The best time to stretch is not before class, but during or after class. Stretches should be slow and steady, not painful.

- Static stretching is recommended as the safest way to gain flexibility, when it's performed correctly. The target muscle(s) should feel a mild to moderate stretch that usually diminishes as the stretch is held. Static stretches should be held for only 30 to 60 seconds and should never be sharp or painful.
- Dynamic stretching, which is often incorporated into ballet class, is another approach. One example of a dynamic stretch would be a grand battement to the front. Here the muscle group being stretched is the hamstrings (in the back of the leg), while the muscle group being engaged is the hip flexors (in the front of the hip). In dynamic stretching it is recommended to start slow and gradually increase the speed and power.
- Ballistic or bouncing stretches can pull or tear muscle fibers and tendons. Muscles reflexively react to quick stretches by tightening up rather than relaxing. We do not recommend this type of stretching for dancers.

SPECIFIC STRETCHES FOR DANCERS

The following are examples of static stretches that are important for every dancer. Although these stretches may seem simple, they should not be neglected or replaced by more elaborate and extreme stretches. Notice that particular attention is being paid to the alignment of the entire body while specific muscle groups are being targeted in the stretch.

PHOTO 24. Lunge Calf Stretch

These stretches are appropriate for the dance teacher to incorporate into class or to recommend to students so that they can do them on their own after class. We realize that dancers and dance teachers may have other, more extreme stretches that they like to do. We recommend that all stretches and movements involving extreme range of motion be supported by muscle contraction. For example: Do not let a student sink into a split on the floor and stay there for a long period of time, over-stretching the muscles and sinking into the joints. Also, extremely flexible or hypermobile dancers should, in particular, be discouraged from doing prolonged stretches in extreme ranges of motion. Instead, they should be encouraged to spend more time on strengthening.

Calf stretch: When dancers stretch their calves consistently, they have fewer calf pulls and Achilles tendon issues.

Lunge Calf Stretch

1. Begin standing in a parallel position with feet hip-width apart, arms lightly placed on the barre. Step back with your right foot and bend your left knee. Your weight should stay in your front leg and your back heel should remain on the floor until you feel a stretch in your calf. You should not feel pain in the Achilles tendon or at the front of the ankle. [See PHOTO 24.]

2. Make sure you keep your pelvis level and pointing straight ahead.

3. Hold for one minute.

4. Next, you can bend the back knee to stretch the soleus muscle (the lower part of your calf).

5. Repeat stretch with the left leg.

Slant Board Calf Stretch

1. Place the right foot on a slant board while the left foot rests on the top of the board. Keep your right heel down, your right knee straight, and make sure your pelvic alignment stays in neutral. [See PHOTO 25.]

2. Hold for one minute.

3. Next, bend the right knee and hold for another minute.

4. You should not feel pain in the Achilles tendon or at the front of the ankle.

5. Repeat stretch with the left leg.

PHOTO 25. Slant Board Calf Stretch

Hamstring and calf stretch, supine and standing:
It is important to stretch the hamstring with the pelvis level instead of always simply raising the leg as high as possible. This focuses specifically on lengthening the hamstring without involving stretching the muscles in the low back.

PHOTO 26. Standing Hamstrings S

Standing Hamstrings Stretch

1. Place your right leg on the barre in parallel directly in front of you with the foot flexed. [See PHOTO 26.]

2. Square off your pelvis, making sure to drop the right hip to be even with the left.

3. Tilt forward from the hip crease (keeping your back straight) until you feel a stretch in your hamstrings.

4. Hold for one minute.

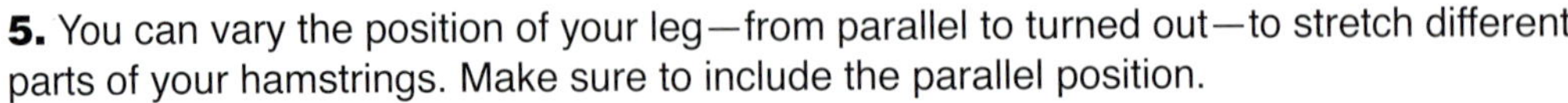

5. You can vary the position of your leg—from parallel to turned out—to stretch different parts of your hamstrings. Make sure to include the parallel position.

6. Repeat stretch with the left leg.

Hamstrings and Calf Stretch (on back)

1. Lie on your back with legs parallel and feet flexed.

2. Looping a strap, belt or towel around your right foot, lift your right leg up until you feel a stretch in your right hamstrings, calf or behind the knee. [See PHOTO 27.] By varying the amount that you flex your foot, you can change where you feel the stretch.

3. Make sure that you are keeping your pelvis level and square. This is not about how high your leg goes. If you are doing the exercise properly, your leg will stop at around 90 degrees.

4. Hold for one minute in different positions to fully stretch out the back of your leg.

5. Repeat with the left leg.

PHOTO 27. Hamstrings and Calf Stretch

Hip external rotators: The deep hip rotators become very tight in dancers because they spend so much time in a turned-out position. This tightness can cause an imbalance in the muscles around the hip.

PHOTO 28. Pretzel Stretch

Pretzel Stretch (for the external rotator muscles in the hips)

1. Sitting on the floor, cross one leg over the other at the knees.

2. Lean forward with a flat back until you feel a stretch in your buttocks. [See PHOTO 28.]

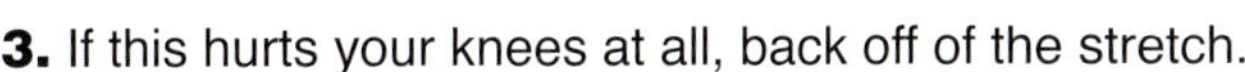

3. If this hurts your knees at all, back off of the stretch.

4. You can also do this stretch on your back, bringing your knees toward your chest.

5. Repeat with the other leg on top.

PHOTO 29. Figure 4 Stretch

Figure 4 Stretch (This stretches the gluteus and its attachment to the iliotibial band.)

1. Place your left lower leg (from knee to ankle) on the barre, with leg turned out and knee bent to 90 degrees. The standing leg is in parallel. [See PHOTO 29.]

2. Pelvis should be square and level.

3. Tilt forward from the hip crease (keeping your back straight) until you feel a stretch in your buttocks or the outside of your thigh.

4. Hold for one minute.

5. Repeat stretch with the right leg.

Alternate position: Lying on your back, cross one ankle over the other knee and bring legs toward your chest.

Hip flexors: It is important to stretch the hip flexors with a neutral or tucked pelvis. This helps stretch the hip for arabesque and takes some of the stress off of the lower back.

Half-Kneel Hip Flexor Stretch

1. Kneel on your left knee. (Make sure to use padding under your left knee and hold the barre or a chair to maintain your balance, if needed.) [See PHOTO 30.]

2. Level off your pelvis and tuck your tailbone under by tightening your buttocks muscles.

PHOTO 30. Hip Flexor Stretch

3. Bend the front knee further, keeping the torso upright, until you feel a stretch in the front outside of your left hip and/or in your left thigh.

4. Hold the position with buttocks tight for 15 seconds and repeat 3-4 times.

5. You can add additional stretch by bending (with port de bras) away from the leg that is stretching.

6. Repeat stretch on right knee.

NOTE: This is not a traditional lunge stretch. You should feel this toward the outside of the front of your hip or in your thigh—not in the groin area.

PHOTO 31. Standing Quad Stre

Quad stretch: Keeping your quads loose is very important to the function of the knee and helps to prevent patellar tendonitis, or jumper's knee.

Standing Quad Stretch

1. Stand in a parallel position with correct posture, then bring your left foot toward your buttocks with your left hand. [See PHOTO 31.]

2. Keep knees together. If you do not feel a stretch in the front of your left thigh, move the left knee backward until you do feel the stretch.

3. You should have no knee pain while doing this stretch.

4. Repeat stretch with the right leg.

PHOTO 32. Half-Kneel Quad Str

Half-Kneel Quad Stretch

1. Kneel on the left knee, and then reach behind you to pull your left foot up to your buttocks. [See PHOTO 32.]

2. You should feel a stretch in the front of your left thigh. If you have any knee pain, stop.

3. Hold position for one minute.

4. Repeat stretch on right leg.

HOW GROWTH SPURTS AFFECT FLEXIBILITY

During growth spurts, bones grow first and muscles and tendons catch up. Growth happens at varying rates, but there will usually be a period of decreased flexibility that can be very disturbing to a young dancer and may result in injuries if the dancer forces the stretch. This period of tightness increases the risk of muscle strains and tendonitis. The dancer should not panic but rather be reassured that it will pass if s/he continues slow, steady stretches. Girls tend to go through their growth spurt between ages 11-13, boys between ages 12-18.

SUGGESTIONS FOR TRAINING DURING GROWTH SPURTS

Develop motor control while decreasing stressors on joints. Use light or no weight for strength training; be careful of a lot of resistance through long lever arms; and do coordination activities that are not extremely challenging physically. For example, instead of focusing on the height of jumps, focus on alignment or on achieving a soft landing. Don't work on increasing the height of leg extensions; work on alignment and the support of the standing leg.

- Educate students about expectations during their growth spurts.
- Develop strength with low resistance, using body weight for resistance (for example, push-ups), and focus on trunk control.
- Maintain or increase appropriate flexibility with regular stretching.
- Focus on creative aspects of dance (for example: musicality, presentation, rhythm, creative development) if the dancer is having a lot of difficulty.
- Consider grouping children according to neuromuscular and musculoskeletal readiness rather than by age alone.

American Ballet Theatre

National Training Curriculum

Health: Part 3

RISK-MANAGEMENT MEDICAL AND FACILITY GUIDELINES

PART 3 CONTRIBUTING AUTHORS
Randall W. Dick, MS, FACSM
Christa Dickey

INTRODUCTION

Part three of the American Ballet Theatre Guidelines for Dancer Health consists of risk-management, medical and facility guidelines for dance schools to consider when developing safety policies and practices. These recommendations are not mandates that must be followed to avoid legal liability or disciplinary sanctions; however, a dance school has a duty to use reasonable care in protecting participants' health and safety while conducting its dance program, and these guidelines may constitute some evidence of the legal standard of care.

RISK MANAGEMENT

A well-managed dance school should maintain the following policies and documents so that proper procedures are in place for optimizing risk management.

1. Create waivers of liability and/or assumption of risk documents.
2. Conduct criminal background checks of employees and contractors who have a responsibility for youth, or have personal contact with dance students.
3. Institute an emergency-response plan, including basic first-aid and instructions for managing emergency cardiac events.

LIABILITY/ASSUMPTION OF RISK

Facilities should provide waivers of liability and/or assumption of risk documents to all facility members and users.

An expressed assumption of risk is a legal document that the dancers and/or parents sign, which indicates that they are aware of the risks associated with their participation in the various physical activity programs offered by the facility. In signing it, they are knowingly accepting full responsibility for their decision to participate in those activities and are releasing the facility from any and all responsibility for their participation. By voluntarily signing a waiver, dancers and parents give up, or waive, their right to institute a claim or litigation. When properly drafted and executed, these documents (the assumption of risk and waiver) are enforceable in most states. But waivers, however appropriate and legal, do not necessarily bar nor preclude a user from filing a claim or from the possibility of litigation if the plaintiff's attorney advises that there is a viable cause of action. Thus, facilities must practice due diligence in the safe delivery of services in accordance with applicable standards and guidelines. An assumption of risk or waiver should be prepared by an attorney and should address the following, at a minimum:

- The facility programs and services to which the dance student has access and which s/he might use to pursue a program of dance.
- The risks involved in participating in any moderate or more intense exercise, including the risk of a cardiac event or even death.
- A statement that the dance student is aware of the risks involved, that the facility has explained those risks thoroughly and that the dance student is willing to accept those risks.
- The dance student's willingness to accept responsibility for participation in light of the information s/he has been given; the dance student's acceptance of complete responsibility for his/her actions; and release of the facility from any and all liability, including the facility's ordinary negligence.

The use of a waiver should be regular practice for all dance facilities. Ideally, all dance students and/or parents should complete and sign a waiver form upon joining a dance facility.

BACKGROUND CHECKS

Facilities should perform criminal background checks on employees and independent contractors who have responsibilities that involve working with youth or having personal contact with dance students or employees in an unsupervised environment.

In many states, this guideline is required by law. In general, employees and independent contractors in the health and fitness industry are actively involved in providing personalized experience that can expose them and the facility to considerable risk. For example, personal trainers, massage therapists, fitness instructors, swim instructors, lifeguards and others work closely with users in a one-on-one environment where risk of an adverse situation exists. Some employees, such as child-care workers, swim instructors, summer camp instructors and tennis instructors, are in positions in which they work closely with young adults and children in a relationship that often involves some authority or control. Jobs in which personal contact might occur are positions for which a facility should consider background checks to ensure that these employees have no prior record of unusual behavior that may expose other employees or dance students to harm. A simple background check, performed by an outside law enforcement agency, can determine if a potential employee or independent contractor has a criminal record that might present risk to other employees or dance students. Background checks can take many forms. As it applies to this guideline, a background check is a process that examines whether an employee or independent contractor has a history of criminal behavior indicating inappropriate behavior with adults or children.

EMERGENCY CARE AND COVERAGE

Unfortunately, reasonable attention to preventive measures will not eliminate all dance injuries. Therefore, each dance school should have an emergency plan in place in case of an injury or accident. A plan is a shared responsibility. Administrators, teachers, parents and medical personnel (when appropriate) should all play a role in the establishment of the plan, the procurement of resources, and assuring and understanding the appropriate emergency response procedures. Components of such a plan should include:

- Planned and immediate access to a medical facility, including a plan for communication and transportation between the dance facility and the medical facility for prompt medical services, when warranted.
- Certain access to a working telephone or other telecommunications device, whether fixed or mobile.
- Keeping all necessary emergency equipment at the site or quickly accessible. Equipment should be in good operating condition, and personnel must be trained in advance to use it properly. Large schools may want to consider having access to an automated external defibrillator (AED)—the device that helps resuscitate someone who is having a cardiac event.
- Encouraging all dance instructors to become certified in cardiopulmonary resuscitation (CPR) techniques, and to be knowledgeable about first aid and the prevention of disease transmission, as outlined by the Occupational Safety and Health Administration (OSHA).
- Having a stocked first-aid kit in a central location. The necessary equipment and/or supplies important for compliance with universal precautions should be available. These supplies include appropriate gloves, disinfectant bleach, antiseptics, bandages and/or dressings. There are many commercially-available first-aid kits, including those that can be obtained from the American Red Cross. In addition to the aforementioned supplies, first-aid kits may contain

alcohol wipes, Band-Aids, butterfly bandages, ammonia inhalants, eye pads, antibiotic ointments, instant cold compresses, hydrocortisone ointments, oral thermometers, scissors and tweezers. Although aspirin tablets and non-aspirin pain relievers are often included in first-aid kits, aspirin should never be given to children and there is a growing consensus that non-aspirin pain relievers should only be taken by children if directed by a physician.

MEDICAL ISSUES

A well-managed dance school should consider the following medical issues when optimizing risk management.

1. Preparticipation medical evaluation or medical history
2. Return to dance after injury or illness
3. Health insurance
4. Injury incident reporting system
5. Skin infections and bleeding
6. General skin infections
7. Cleaning blood spills and OPIM

PREPARTICIPATION MEDICAL EVALUATION (PME)

Before dance students take on the rigors of any organized activity, their health should be evaluated by qualified medical personnel. Such an examination should determine whether the dance students are medically cleared to engage in dance-related activities.

The following information generally applies to the medical evaluations of students in traditional educational institutions. It is provided here as informational background for dance schools. It should be noted that dance schools in general are not required to conduct preparticipation examinations. Nonetheless, the dance school should make every effort to be aware of any medical conditions that may adversely affect its dance students.

Special Concerns for Girls

It is important to ask female dancers questions regarding the female athlete triad (disordered eating, osteoporosis and amenorrhea—see Part 2) as well as the use of weight-control medications. A female dancer who has suffered from a stress fracture should have a nutrition consultation and menstrual function evaluation.

Special Concerns for Boys

Male dancers need to be questioned about the use of anabolic steroids and other performance-enhancing drugs, as well as weight gain products (see “Nutrition/Dietary Supplements” and “Substance Abuse” in Part 2).

MEDICAL HISTORY

It is advisable that dancers with health issues that might impact their dance activities truthfully disclose their relevant medical history to their dance school. This information can be used to assess a dancer's ability to participate in dance class/performance.

RETURN TO DANCE AFTER INJURY OR ILLNESS

For those dancers who have sustained a significant injury or illness that impacted their ability to participate in dance activities, it is advisable that a letter of medical clearance from the dancer's physician be kept on file at the dance facility. This will document any conditions or limitations as they relate to the dancer's participation in dance activities.

HEALTH INSURANCE

Dance students should be covered by individual, parental or institutional medical insurance to defray the costs associated with a significant injury or illness.

INJURY INCIDENT REPORTING SYSTEM

Dance studios should keep a record of all injuries and accidents that occur at their facility and evaluate the data annually to minimize future risk.

SKIN INFECTIONS AND BLEEDING

Dance schools should ensure that policies exist for orientation and staff education on the prevention and transmission of skin infections and blood-borne pathogens. In 1992, the Occupational Safety and Health Administration (OSHA) developed a standard directed at eliminating or minimizing occupational exposure to blood-borne pathogens. Each dance school should determine the applicability of the OSHA standard to its personnel and facilities.

GENERAL SKIN INFECTIONS

Prevention of general skin infections can be aided through proper routine cleaning of all equipment, including floors, barres and shared areas, such as locker rooms. Skin infections can be transmitted by both direct (person to person) and indirect (person one—to surface—to person two) contact. Suggested preventive measures include: washing hands; not picking, squeezing or scratching skin lesions; showering after activities; not sharing towels; and regular cleaning of shared facilities. (For more: see Part 2).

CLEANING BLOOD SPILLS AND OPIM

All individuals responsible for cleaning and disinfection of blood spills or Other Potentially Infectious Materials (OPIM) should be trained regarding proper procedures and the use of universal precautions.

- Assemble and maintain equipment and/or supplies for treating injured/bleeding dancers. Items may include: antiseptics, antimicrobial wipes, bandages and waste receptacles appropriate for soiled equipment—dancewear, towels and other waste. Personal Protective Equipment (PPE) such as gloves should always be at the ready. Large dance schools might also consider having goggles and a mask on hand, although they likely will not be needed.
- All dance facilities should have a first-aid kit on hand and should be prepared to treat any wounds, abrasions or cuts that may serve as a source of bleeding or as a port of entry for blood-borne pathogens or other potentially infectious organisms. Wounds should be covered with a bandage that is air- and water-tight and will withstand the demands of dance activities. Likewise, care providers with healing wounds or dermatitis (skin inflammations) should have these areas adequately covered to prevent transmission to or from a dancer. Dancers may be advised to wear more protective equipment on high-risk areas, such as elbows and hands.
- When a dance student is bleeding, the bleeding must be stopped and the open wound covered. Dancers with active bleeding should be removed from the dance activity as soon as is practical.
- Dance students must be aware of their responsibility to report a bleeding wound to the instructor.
- Personnel managing a blood exposure must follow the guidelines for universal precaution. Gloves, and if necessary other Personal Protective Equipment (PPE), should be worn for direct contact with blood or other body fluids. Gloves should be changed after treating each individual dancer. After removing and discarding gloves, hands should be washed.
- If blood or body fluids are transferred from an injured or bleeding dancer to the intact skin of another dancer, the activity must be stopped, the skin cleaned with antimicrobial wipes to remove gross contaminants, and the participant instructed to wash with soap and water as soon as possible. Antimicrobial wipes are commercially available wipes that contain such things as isopropyl alcohol or benzalkonium.

FACILITY ISSUES

A well-managed dance school should consider the following facility guidelines for participants when optimizing risk management.

FACILITIES, EQUIPMENT AND VENTILATION

Dance facilities provide space specifically for the pursuit of dance-related activities and may have one or more dance studios, a reception area, locker rooms, a lounge area, a physical therapy room, and a Pilates or fitness room. Dance facilities should have physical activity spaces as well as non-activity spaces. Both should provide sufficient space to accommodate the expected number of people (dancers, teachers, parents, etc.).

The adequacy and conditions of the facilities used for dance instruction should not be overlooked, and periodic examination of the facilities should be conducted. Inspection of the facilities should include not only the performance area, but also warm-up and adjacent areas.

Purchasers of equipment (for example, barres, floors, mirrors, etc.) should be aware of and use safety standards. In addition, attention should be directed to maintaining proper repair and fitting of equipment at all times. Dance students should be instructed to notify their dance teachers when equipment appears to be unsafe.

FLOORS

When dancers work in dance class or perform, their bodies are exposed to an enormous amount of stress. The act of jumping and landing causes intensified pressure on the lower extremities, but many simpler exercises—basic pointe work, relevé/plié, lifts for men—can cause stress as well. Fortunately, through the proper design and installation of a dance floor surface, many of these additional forces can be absorbed by the floor surface rather than by the individual's musculoskeletal system.

The primary role served by properly designed and constructed floors is the reduction of injuries that could occur in dance class. Normally, these floors have a three-layer system consisting of a bottom shock-absorbing layer (neoprene shock pads, rubber pads and springs), a middle layer that has two layers of plywood, and a top layer consisting of a wood, rubber or Marley surface.

Facilities should adhere to the Deutsches Institut fur Normung (DIN) standards when installing dance floors (www.din.de). Dance facility operators should discuss their facility's requirements with dance floor manufacturers to ensure that the floors that they select for their facility are constructed in accordance with DIN standards.

BARRES

In order for a ballet student to feel properly aligned and comfortable at the barre, it is important that the barre not be too tall or too short. The standard heights for all ballet barres (mounted to the wall or portable) are: 42 inches for adults, 36 inches for children.

VENTILATION

Dance facilities should provide all physical activity spaces with sufficient air circulation and fresh (outside) air, which will allow the facility to maintain air quality, room temperatures and humidity at safe and comfortable levels during times of physical activity.

Air circulation is one of the most critical elements when designing and operating a dance facility. When a room is filled with dancers exercising at moderate to high intensity, the heat and humidity load increases dramatically. This can place an increased level of heat stress on the dancers and may result in dehydration, heat exhaustion, heatstroke or (in rare instances) cardiovascular emergencies. In addition to the increased heat load that can result from improper air circulation, poor air quality can expose dancers to airborne pathogens and increase the risk of respiratory disorders or other airborne illnesses. Facilities can provide sufficient air circulation by taking into consideration the following factors:

- Maintain relative humidity at 60% or lower in all physical activity spaces.
- If possible, maintain air temperature for all physical activity areas between 68 and 72 degrees F, or 20 and 23 degrees C.
- Ensure that wet areas, such as shower areas, steam rooms and whirlpool areas, have a negative exhaust system. A negative exhaust system allows air to be pulled out of these moist areas rather than stagnating there.
- Keep the mechanical system clean. This preventive maintenance will allow the system to provide better air circulation and will also prevent the buildup of dirt and microbes in the system.
- Make sure that there is an adequate mix of external fresh air and recirculated internal air moving through the facility. The higher the percentage of external air, the less likely the system will circulate air that contains airborne pathogens that were released by those who use the facility.

CLEANING OF FACILITIES AND FLOORS

Below is a table that lists the recommended cleaning and disinfecting procedures for fitness and group exercise facilities.

Recommended Cleaning Procedures

CLEANING ACTIVITY	FREQUENCY
Remove trash	Daily
Dry-mop wood and/or marley floors	Daily
Dust all horizontal surfaces	Daily
Spot-clean mirrors and glass surfaces	Daily
Wash and disinfect rubber floor surfaces	Daily
Wet-mop wood and/or marley floors	Daily
Clean mirrors thoroughly	Weekly
Clean HVAC ducts	Bimonthly
Clean light fixtures	Bimonthly
Clean audio equipment	Bimonthly
Wash solid walls	Quarterly or annually
Refinish wood floor surfaces	Annually

Marley Floors: Marley flooring is maintained by wet-mopping daily with hot water only and mopping once a week with a 1 to 10 solution of ammonia and hot water or rubbing alcohol and hot water. Scuffmarks, shoe dyes and rosin build-up can be removed by sprinkling rubbing alcohol directly onto the marks and dry-mopping. Contact your dance floor supplier to receive specific cleaning and maintenance guidelines for products.

Ballet Barres: There are no universal standards for disinfecting barres. Generally, studios increase cleaning frequency depending on class size and season. An alcohol wipe is sometimes used but any disinfectant—such as bleach or rubbing alcohol diluted with water—can be used.

RESOURCES TO FIND HEALTH PROFESSIONALS WITH DANCE EXPERTISE

For information regarding medical professionals with backgrounds in dance, the following organizations may be contacted:

- American College of Sports Medicine (ACSM) has members with dance medicine expertise (in research and/or practice), www.acsm.org
- American Association of Orthopedic Surgeons (AAOS), www.aaos.org
- American Orthopedic Society for Sports Medicine (AOSSM), www.sportsmed.org
- American Medical Society for Sports Medicine (AMSSM), www.newamssm.org
- Certified professionals (ACSM ProFinder) for health and fitness training in specific geographic locations, www.acsm.org
- International Association for Dance Medicine and Science (IADMS), www.iadms.org

SOURCE MATERIAL

PART 2: DEVELOPMENT AND HEALTH

CHAPTER 8: Motor Control and Learning

Articles

Calvo-Merino B, Glaser DE, Grèzes J, Passingham RE and Haggard P: "Action Observation and Acquired Motor Skills: An fMRI Study with Expert Dancers." Cerebral Cortex, 15(8):1243, 2005.

Carr S and Wyon M: "The Impact of Motivational Climate on Dance Students' Achievement Goals, Trait Anxiety and Perfectionism." Journal of Dance Medicine & Science, 7(4):105, 2003.

Enghauser R: "Motor Learning and the Dance Technique Class." Journal of Dance Education, 3(3):85, 2003.

Farrar-Baker A and Wilmerding MV: "Prevalence of Lateral Bias in the Teaching of Beginning and Advanced Ballet." (Abstract) Journal of Dance Medicine & Science, 10(3&4), 2006.

Gray JT, Neisser U, Shapiro BA and Kouns S: "Observational Learning of Ballet Sequences: The Role of Kinematic Information." Ecological Psychology, 3:121, 1991.

Ramsay JRE and Riddich MJ: "Professional Ballet Dancers Perform With Outstanding Accuracy." Clinical Rehabilitation, 15:324, 2001.

Wilmerding MV, Heyward VH, King M, Fiedler KJ, Stidley C and Evans B: "Electromyographical Comparison of the Developpé Devant at Barre and Centre." Journal of Dance Medicine & Science, 5(3):69, 2001.

Books

Clarkson PM and Skrinar M (eds.): The Science of Dance Training. Champaign, IL: Human Kinetics Books, 1988.

Gallahue DL and Ozmun JC: Understanding Motor Development. Dubuque, IA: Brown & Benchmark, 1995.

CHAPTER 9: Phases of Development

Adapted from The USA Gymnastics Athlete Wellness Book, Pilot Edition, Official text for USA Gymnastics Athlete Wellness Course. Edited and Co-Authored by Thies-Marshall N. Contributing authors: Balague G, Larsen L and Strawbridge M. Indianapolis, IN: USA Gymnastics Publications, 1998.

CHAPTER 10: Psychological and Emotional Factors of Dance Training

Adapted from The USA Gymnastics Athlete Wellness Book, Pilot Edition, Official text for USA Gymnastics Athlete Wellness Course. Edited and Co-Authored by Thies-Marshall N. Contributing authors: Balague G, Larsen L and Strawbridge M. Indianapolis, IN: USA Gymnastics Publications, 1998.

Burnout

Gould D: Foundations of Sport and Exercise Psychology, 4 Rev Ed. Human Kinetics Europe Ltd (United States), 2006.

Raglin JS: "Exercise and Mental Health. Beneficial and Detrimental Effects." Sports Med, 9(6):323, 1990.

Drug Abuse

Wadler GI: "The Coach and Athlete Drug Abuse." Olympic Coach, 6(1):9, Winter 1996.

Wadler GI and Hainline B: Drugs and the Athlete. Philadelphia: FA Davis Company, 1989.

Eating Disorders

Adapted from the National Collegiate Athletic Association's (NCAA) Sports Medicine Handbook, 2006-07. www.ncaa.org

Female Athlete Triad

Nattiv A, Loucks AB, Manore MM, Sanborn CF, Sundgot-Borgen J and Warren MP: "American College of Sports Medicine Position Stand: The Female Athlete Triad." American College of Sports Medicine, Medicine and Science in Sports and Exercise, 39(10):1867, 2007.

Menstrual Cycle

Adapted from the National Collegiate Athletic Association's (NCAA) Sports Medicine Handbook, 2006-07. www.ncaa.org

ADDITIONAL RESOURCES

American Academy of Pediatrics Committee on Sports Medicine: "Amenorrhea in Adolescent Athletes." Pediatrics, 84(2):394, 1989.

Keen AD and Drinkwater BL: "Irreversible Bone Loss in Former Amenorrheic Athletes." Osteoporosis International, 7(4):311, 1997.

Loucks AB, Verdun M and Heath EM: "Low Energy Availability, Not Stress of Exercise, Alters LH Pulsatility in Exercising Women." Journal of Applied Physiology, 84(1):37, 1998.

Mellion MB, Putakian CC and Madden CC (eds): "Sports Medicine Secrets." Medicine Secrets, 3rd edition, 2003.

Otis CT, Drinkwater BL, Johnson M, Loucks AB and Wilmore J: "American College of Sports Medicine Position Stand on the Female Athlete Triad." Medicine and Science in Sports and Exercise, 29(5): i-ix, 1997.

Shangold M, Rebar RW, Wentz AC and Schiff I: "Evaluation and Management of Menstrual Dysfunction in Athletes." Journal of American Medical Association, 262(12):1665, 1990.

"Clinics in Sports Medicine." The Athletic Woman, April 2000.

Peer Pressure

Adapted from USA Swimming's National Age Group Camp Parents Manual, LSC Racing Camp. www.usaswimming.org

CHAPTER 13: Principles of Training

Strength Training

Berardi G: Finding Balance: Fitness, Training and Health for a Lifetime in Dance, Second Edition. NY: Routledge, 2005.

Clippinger K: "Supplemental Strength Training For Young Dancers." Journal of Dance Medicine & Science, 2(2):74, 1998.

Fitt SS: Dance Kinesiology. NY: Schirmer Books, 1988.

Geeves T: "A Report on Dance Injury Prevention and Management in Australia." The Australian Association for Dance Education in association with The National Arts Industry Training Council, March 1990.

McArdle WD, Katch FI and Katch VL: Essentials of Exercise Physiology, Fifth Edition. Lippincott, Williams & Wilkins, January 2001.

McArdle WD, Katch FI and Katch VL: Exercise Physiology: Energy, Nutrition and Human Performance, Third Edition. PA: Lea & Febiger, 1991.

Phillips C: "Strength Training of Dancers During the Adolescent Growth Spurt." Journal of Dance Medicine & Science, 3(2):66, 1999.

Ryan AJ and Stephens RE (eds): The Healthy Dancer: Dance Medicine for Dancers. NJ: Princeton Book Company, 1987.

ADDENDUM TO STRENGTH TRAINING

Adapted from the National Strength and Conditioning Association's (NSCA) Youth Resistance Training: Position Statement Paper and Literature Review: Strength and Conditioning: Vol. 18, No. 6, pp. 62–76. Faigenbaum AD, Kraemer WJ, Cahill B, Chandler J, Dziados J, Elfrink LD, Forman E, Gaudiose M, Micheli L, Nitka M and Roberts S, 1996.
www.nsca-lift.org

PART 3: RISK-MANAGEMENT, MEDICAL AND FACILITY GUIDELINES

The American College of Sports Medicine's (ACSM) Health/Fitness Facility Standards and Guidelines, Third Edition. Tharrett SJ, McInnis KJ and Peterson JA (eds.), 2007.
www.acsm.org

The National Collegiate Athletic Association (NCAA) Sports Medicine Handbook, Eighteenth Edition. Compiled by: Klossner D, Associate Director of Education Outreach. August 2006. Copyright 2006, by the National Collegiate Athletic Association. Printed in the United States of America.
www.ncaa.org

INDEX

Index

Index

MEDICAL ADVISORY BOARD BIOGRAPHIES

Gary I. Wadler, MD, FACP, FACSM, FACPM, FCP (Chairman), a clinical associate professor of medicine at New York University School of Medicine, is an internist and sports medicine physician with special expertise in the field of drug abuse in sports.The lead author of the internationally acclaimed textbook *Drugs and the Athlete*, Dr. Wadler is an active member of the World Anti-Doping Agency (WADA), where he chairs its Prohibited List and Method Committee and serves on its Health, Medicine and Research Committee. In 1993, he received the International Olympic Committee's President's Prize, and in 2007, he was selected as "One of the 100 Most Influential Sports Educators in America." Dr. Wadler has served as a medical advisor to the White House Office of National Drug Control Policy, as a trustee of the Board of the American College of Sports Medicine, and as a trustee and vice-president of the Women's Sports Foundation. He was tournament physician for the US Open Tennis Championships for 11 years and was the founder of the Health and Medical Committee of the Women's Tennis Association. Dr. Wadler is chairman of the College Council of the State of New York at Old Westbury and is chairman of the Nassau County Sports Commission in New York. He maintains a private practice in Internal Medicine and Sports Medicine in Manhasset, New York.

Phillip A. Bauman, MD, is a board-certified orthopedic surgeon who has specialized in the treatment of dance-related injuries since 1987. He is an orthopedic consultant to The American Ballet Theatre, The Jacqueline Kennedy Onassis School at American Ballet Theatre, ABT II, New York City Ballet, the School of American Ballet at Lincoln Center and many other dance groups, companies and Broadway shows. Dr. Bauman has served on the advisory boards of *Pointe* and *Dance Teacher* magazines. Currently, he is a senior attending physician in orthopedic surgery at St. Luke's–Roosevelt Hospital Center in New York City, holds an academic appointment at the College of Physicians and Surgeons at Columbia University, and is a fellow of the American Academy of Orthopaedic Surgeons.

Lisa R. Callahan, MD, is medical director of the Women's Sports Medicine Center at the Hospital for Special Surgery and the director of player care for the New York Knicks and Liberty basketball teams. She is board certified in family medicine and holds a CAQ in sports medicine. She is an associate professor of clinical medicine in the Department of Medicine at Weill Medical College of Cornell University and a member of the Board of Directors of the American Medical Society for Sports Medicine (AMSSM). She is a contributing editor to *Self* magazine and author of *The Fitness Factor: Every Woman's Key to a Lifetime of Health and Well-being.*

Priscilla M. Clarkson, PhD, is a distinguished professor of kinesiology and currently serves as dean of Commonwealth College, the honors college at the University of Massachusetts, Amherst. She has served as president of the New England Regional American College of Sports Medicine (ACSM) Chapter, president of the National ACSM, and president of the ACSM Foundation. Professor Clarkson served as the editor of the *International Journal of Sport Nutrition and Exercise Metabolism* for eight years, serves on the editorial or advisory boards for several other scientific journals, and is currently editor-in-chief of *Exercise and Sport Science Reviews.* In 2005, she received the National ACSM Honor Award and the University of Massachusetts Award for Outstanding Accomplishments in Research or Creative Activity. Professor Clarkson has authored and edited two books in the area of Dance Medicine.

Julie Daugherty, MPT is the New York–based physical therapist for American Ballet Theatre, ABT II and the JKO school. Prior to joining ABT, she worked with Merce Cunningham Dance Company and on staff at the Harkness Center for Dance Injuries, where she also served as on-site physical therapist for Dance Theatre of Harlem. Ms. Daugherty taught anatomy and injury prevention classes to young dancers at Dance Theatre of Harlem and the Feld Ballet's Ballet Tech. Her lumbar stabilization research was published in the *Journal of Orthopaedic and Sports Physical Therapy* and her pediatric dance research was presented at the American Physical Therapy Association's 2000 Combined Sections Meeting.

Franco De Vita is Principal of ABT Jacqueline Kennedy Onassis School. He danced with several European ballet companies, and also performed in musical comedies and operettas. When he retired from the stage, Mr. De Vita earned teaching qualifications, acquiring the Enrico Cecchetti Diploma and the highest teaching degree given by the Italian Ministry of Education. Mr. De Vita has taught for ABT, ABT II, The Ailey School and Company, and was Dean of Faculty and Curriculum at Boston Ballet School. Together with Raymond Lukens, Mr. De Vita directed the Hamlyn School of Dance in Florence, Italy.

Randall W. Dick, MS, FACSM, works as associate director of the Research/Injury Surveillance System at the National Collegiate Athletic Association. Since 1987, he has been a liaison to the NCAA Committee on Competitive Safeguards and Medical Aspects of Sports, working with sports medicine issues. In January 2003, he left his committee liaison role to direct the Association's efforts to develop a web-based injury data collection system including accessibility to and application of the resulting data. Mr. Dick represents the NCAA on the NATA College/University Athletic Trainers' Association, is a fellow in the American College of Sports Medicine and is a member of the United States Lacrosse Sports Sciences Committee.

Christa Dickey is the director of communications at the American College of Sports Medicine (ACSM), where she manages media relations and public information for the world's largest sports medicine and exercise science association. Ms. Dickey works with physicians, researchers and educators from a variety of health and fitness disciplines to create tools for the public and translate medical studies and research. She also acts as liaison to many programs and initiatives, primarily in clinical sports medicine and youth sports and health. Among these activities, she works closely with federal health agencies, sports leagues and organizations, and medical associations on health, fitness and wellness communications and public education objectives.

James G. Garrick, MD, is an orthopedic surgeon and the founder and director of the Center for Sports Medicine in San Francisco, California, as well as the founder of the Sports Medicine Division at the University of Washington. He also is a founding member and former board member of the American Orthopaedic Society for Sports Medicine. He is a clinical professor in the Department of Pediatrics at the University of California, San Francisco. Dr. Garrick currently serves on the editorial boards of *The American Journal of Sports Medicine, Medical Problems of Performing Artists* and *The Journal of Orthopaedic & Sports Physical Therapy.* Recently, Dr. Garrick was named editor-in-chief of *The Journal of Dance Medicine & Science.*

William G. Hamilton, MD, BSE, AAOS, FACS, is a board-certified orthopedic surgeon, practicing in New York City. He is a member of the American Academy of Orthopaedic Surgeons and a fellow of the American College of Surgeons. He is a past president of The American Orthopaedic Foot & Ankle Society (AOFAS) and The New York Medical and Surgical Society. He is the orthopedic surgeon for American Ballet Theatre, ABT II and The Jacqueline Kennedy Onassis School at ABT, as well as New York City Ballet and The School of American Ballet at Lincoln Center. His interest in the field began when George Balanchine asked him to take care of NYCB in 1972 and Mikhail Baryshnikov asked him to take care of ABT in 1980. He is clinical professor of Orthopedic Surgery at Columbia University, College of Physicians and Surgeons.

Raymond Lukens is Artistic Associate of the ABT/New York University Masters Degree Program, for which he created the ballet pedagogy syllabi. He is a faculty member of ABT Jacqueline Kennedy Onassis School and has taught for ABT and ABT II. As a performer, Mr. Lukens toured extensively dancing works by Van Dyk, Balanchine, Petipa and Bournonville, among others. Before joining ABT, Mr. Lukens was director of Boston Ballet II and ballet master for Boston Ballet, and the ballet companies in Hartford, Cincinnati and Calgary's Alberta Ballet.

Peter Marshall, MA, PT, graduated with honors with a degree in physical therapy from Ithaca College and obtained his Master's Degree in physical therapy from New York University. Mr. Marshall founded the physical therapy program at American Ballet Theatre in 1983 and has directed the program since its inception. He has authored multiple articles on dance-related injuries and treatment that have been published internationally in a variety of juried medical journals. Mr. Marshall also served as the physical therapist for Baryshnikov Productions from 1983-1993.

Kevin McKenzie was appointed Artistic Director of ABT in October 1992. He is an alumnus of ABT, as well as the National Ballet of Washington and The Joffrey Ballet. His choreographic credits include: *Groupo Zamboria* (1984) and *Transcendental Études* (1991), both created for Martine van Hamel's New Amsterdam Ballet; *Lucy and the Count* (1992) for The Washington Ballet; and the full-length classics *The Nutcracker* (1993) and *Don Quixote* (1995), in collaboration with Susan Jones, and the new productions of *Swan Lake* and *Sleeping Beauty*, all for ABT.

Lyle J. Micheli, MD, former president of the American College of Sports Medicine, is the co-founder and director of sports medicine at Boston Children's Hospital and associate clinical professor of orthopedic surgery at Harvard Medical School. He also serves as orthopedist for the Boston Ballet and the American Rugby Association. Dr. Micheli is currently the vice president of the International Federation of Sports Medicine and has served as chairman of the Massachusetts Governor's Council on Fitness and Sports. Dr. Micheli is the author of hundreds of published clinical studies and scholarly review articles and books.

Rachel S. Moore is an alumna of ABT's corps de ballet. She was named Executive Director of American Ballet Theatre in April 2004. She currently teaches in the Arts Administration program at Columbia University, and she recently received a Distinguished Alumni Award from Columbia University's Teacher's College. She also serves on the boards of Project STEP, Dance/USA and the National Dance Foundation of Bermuda, and is a member of the United States National Commission for UNESCO and the Advisory Committee of Dance/NYC.

Caroline Silby, PhD, MEd, holds a Doctorate and Master's Degree in Sports Psychology from the University of Virginia. She is a nationally recognized expert on the development of young female athletes, author of *Games Girls Play: Understanding and Guiding Young Female Athletes* (St. Martin's Press) and adjunct faculty member at American University. Dr. Silby has worked on an individual basis with a number of Olympians and National Competitors. Currently, Dr. Silby serves on the Board of the Kindness Counts Foundation, is an advisor to the Center for Sports Parenting, assists the Women's Sports Foundation as a member of their Advisory Council and is a consultant to the American Girl Company.

Eric Small, MD, FAAP, is a nationally recognized expert in Pediatric/Adolescent Sports Medicine, and is one of only a handful of physicians in the United States with this concentrated specialty. He has private practice locations in New York City and Westchester County, New York. His areas of clinical expertise include: sports injury management, reflex sympathetic dystrophy, exertional leg pain and educational programming regarding steroids and nutritional supplements. Dr. Small is the former chairman of the American Academy of Pediatrics Committee on Sports Medicine and Fitness and serves as a medical consultant to Girl Scouts of America and The Center for Sports Parenting. He is clinical assistant professor of Pediatrics, Orthopedics and Rehabilitation Medicine at Mount Sinai School of Medicine in New York, and is founder and director of Family Sports Medicine & Nutrition of New York. Dr. Small is founder and former chairperson of the United States Tennis Association/Eastern Section Sports Science Committee.

Angela D. Smith, MD, an orthopedic surgeon at the Children's Hospital of Philadelphia and its Sports Medicine and Performance Center, is a past president of the American College of Sports Medicine (ACSM). She currently chairs the Education Commission of the International Federation of Sports Medicine (FIMS), coordinating and teaching courses for health professionals worldwide. Through her clinical practice and educational efforts she aims to improve each person's physical fitness, to improve health, performance and self-esteem, and to prevent injury. Her recent quotes have appeared in *The New York Times* and a front-page *Wall Street Journal* article, as well as NBC's national evening news featuring the hinged figure skating boot that she co-developed. She has also served as United States Figure Skating World Team and World Junior Team physician.

Virginia Wilmerding, PhD, was president of the International Association for Dance Medicine & Science (IADMS) from 2005-2007. She danced professionally for a number of modern dance companies in New York City before moving to New Mexico, where she is now an adjunct professor at the University of New Mexico. She has published original research in *Journal of Dance Medicine & Science, Medical Problems of Performing Artists, Medicine and Science in Sports & Exercise, Journal of Strength and Conditioning Research* and *Idea Today.* Research interests include body composition, training methodologies, injury incidence and prevention, pedagogical considerations in technique class, and the physiological requirements of various dance idioms.